FAVORITE FILET CROCHET DESIGNS

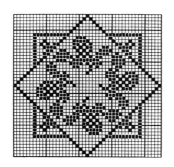

Edited by

RITA WEISS

DOVER PUBLICATIONS, INC., NEW YORK

CROCHET ABBREVIATIONS

ch	chain	**pc st**	popcorn stitch
sc	single crochet	**sp**	space
half dc	half double crochet	**st(s)**	stitch(es)
dc	double crochet	**rnd**	round
tr	treble	**incl**	inclusive
d tr	double treble	**inc**	increase
sl st	slip stitch	**dec**	decrease

*(asterisk) or † (dagger) . . . Repeat the instructions following the asterisk or dagger as many times as specified.

** or ÷ ÷ . . . Used for a second set of repeats within one set of instructions.

Repeat instructions in parentheses as many times as specified. For example: "**(Ch 5, sc in next sc) 5 times**" means to work all that is in parentheses 5 times.

Copyright © 1985 by Dover Publications, Inc.
All rights reserved under Pan American and International Copyright Conventions.

Published in Canada by General Publishing Company, Ltd., 30 Lesmill Road, Don Mills, Toronto, Ontario.
Published in the United Kingdom by Constable and Company, Ltd., 10 Orange Street, London WC2H 7EG.

This Dover edition, first published in 1985, is a new selection of patterns from *Bedspreads, Book No. 122*, published by The Spool Cotton Company in 1938; *Hand Crochet by Royal Society, Book No. 1*, published by Royal Society, Inc., in 1943; *Home Favorites in Crochet, Book No. 214*, published by The Clark Thread Company in 1944; *Filet Crochet, Book No. 193*, published by The Spool Cotton Company in 1943; *Hand Crochet by Royal Society, Book No. 6, Table Settings*, published by Royal Society, Inc., in 1946; *Table Treasures, Book No. 152*, published by The Spool Cotton Company in 1940; *Doilies, Lily Design Book No. 79*, published by Lily Mills Company in 1956; *Royal Society Designs for Crochet, Book No. 36*, published by the Frampton Company in 1934; *New Ideas in Crochet, Table Topics, Book No. 123*, published by The Spool Cotton Company in 1938; *Tablecloths, Book No. 231*, published by The Spool Cotton Company in 1947; *Crocheted Tablecloths and Luncheon Sets, Book No. 179*, published by The Spool Cotton Company in 1942. A new introduction has been specially written for this edition.

Manufactured in the United States of America
Dover Publications, Inc., 31 East 2nd Street, Mineola, N.Y. 11501

Library of Congress Cataloging in Publication Data
Main entry under title:

Favorite filet crochet designs.

(Dover needlework series)
1. Crocheting—Patterns. I. Weiss, Rita. II. Series.
TT820.F348 1985   746.2'2   85-6844
ISBN 0-486-24930-1

Introduction

Among the favorite old crochet techniques that have re-appeared over the past few years is the fascinating craft of filet crochet. Originally developed as an easy and inexpensive means of creating filet lace (a lace with geometric designs made by darning patterns on a square mesh ground), filet crochet is enjoyed by crocheters because it allows them to create pictures by the simple means of crocheting open and closed squares.

This book is a collection of beautiful filet crochet designs published in instruction leaflets produced by America's thread companies during the first half of this century. During this period, the large thread companies employed huge staffs to create new designs and produce new leaflets solely as a method of merchandising their thread. As the rage for crocheted items disappeared, so did the leaflets. The thread companies began to concentrate on products other than crochet thread, and the instructional books disappeared or were destroyed.

With the resurgence of interest in handmade items, crocheted lace has once again emerged as a popular craft. Crocheters are therefore anxiously searching for more and more designs. The old leaflets, complete with magnificent designs and instructions, and the filet projects they inspired have become collector's items.

Modern technology permits us to reproduce these instructions exactly as they appeared in those original old leaflets. Many of the threads listed with the patterns are still available. If not, other threads that will produce the same gauge can be purchased. Always check with your local needlework shop or department; you may find that the name of a given thread now being sold is the same as in these old instructions, but the thread itself is different. Whatever type of thread you decide to use, be certain to buy sufficient thread of the same dye lot to complete the project you wish to make. It is often impossible to match shades later, as dye lots vary.

For perfect results the number of stitches and rows should correspond with that indicated in the directions. Before starting a project, make a small sample of the stitch, working with the suggested hook size and desired thread. If your working tension is too tight or too loose, use a larger or smaller crochet hook to obtain the correct gauge.

When you have finished your project, wash and block it. No matter how carefully you have worked, blocking will give your filet work a more "professional" look. Use a good neutral soap or detergent and make suds in cool water. Wash by squeezing the suds through the filet crochet project, but do not rub. Rinse two or three times in clear water. Starching the work will give it a crisper look. Using rustproof pins, pin the work right side down on a well-padded surface. When the project is almost dry, press through a damp cloth with a moderately hot iron. Do not rest the iron on the filet crochet. Let the steam do the work! When thoroughly dry, remove the pins.

The crochet terminology and hooks listed in this book are those used in the United States. The following charts give the U.S. names of crochet stitches and their equivalents in other countries and the equivalents to U.S. crochet hook sizes. Crocheters should become thoroughly familiar with the differences in both crochet terms and hook sizes before starting any project.

All of the stitches used in the projects in this book are explained on page 47. A metric conversion chart is located on page 48.

STITCH CONVERSION CHART

U.S. Name	Equivalent
Chain	Chain
Slip	Single crochet
Single crochet	Double crochet
Half-double or short-double crochet	Half-treble crochet
Double crochet	Treble crochet
Treble crochet	Double-treble crochet
Double-treble crochet	Treble-treble crochet
Treble-treble or long-treble crochet	Quadruple-treble crochet
Afghan stitch	Tricot crochet

HOOK CONVERSION CHART

Aluminum

U.S. Size	B	C	D	E	F	G	H	I	J	K
British & Canadian Size	12	11	10	9	8	7	5	4	3	2
Metric Size	2½	3	—	3½	4	4½	5	5½	6	7

Steel

U.S. Size	00	0	1	2	3	4	5	6
British & Canadian Size	000	00	0	1	—	1½	2	2½

ORCHID FILET TABLECLOTH

A REALLY SUMPTUOUS CLOTH FOR SPECIAL OCCASIONS

What You Need:

ROYAL SOCIETY SIX CORD CORDICHET

Small Ball, size 50: 107 balls.

Steel Crochet Hook No. 12.

Tablecloth measures about 75 x 90 inches.

GAUGE: 9 sps make 2 inches; 9 rows make 2 inches. Square measures about 15 x 15 inches.

SQUARE . . . Starting at bottom of chart, make a chain about 20 inches long (18 ch sts to 1 inch). **1st row:** Dc in 5th ch from hook, tr in next 4 ch (1 bl made); ch 3, sk 3 ch, tr in next ch (1 sp made); tr in next 16 ch; * (ch 1, sk 1 ch, tr in next ch) twice (1 shadow sp made); (ch 3, sk 3 ch, tr in next ch) 5 times; (ch 1, sk 1 ch, tr in next ch) twice; tr in next 12 ch. Repeat from * once more. 1 shadow sp, 4 sps, 1 shadow sp, 4 bls, 1 shadow sp, 4 sps, (1 shadow sp, 3 bls, 1 shadow sp, 5 sps) twice; 1 shadow sp, 4 bls, 1 sp, 1 bl. Cut off remaining ch. Ch 7, turn. **2nd row:** Sk 3 tr, tr in next tr (1 sp over bl made); 3 tr in next sp, tr in next tr (1 bl over sp made); tr in next 12 tr; (ch 1, sk 1 tr, tr in next tr) twice (1 shadow sp over bl made); (tr in next sp, tr in next tr) twice (1 bl over shadow sp made); (ch 1, tr in next sp, ch 1, tr in next tr) 5 times (5 shadow sps over 5 sps made); make 1 bl, (3 shadow sps, 1 bl, 5 shadow sps, 1 bl) twice; 2 shadow sps, 1 bl, 5 shadow sps (1 bl, 3 shadow sps, 1 bl, 5 shadow sps) twice; 1 bl, 1 shadow sp, 4 bls, ch 3, tr in 4th st of turning ch. Ch 4, turn.

3rd row: 4 bls, 1 shadow sp, ch 3, sk next tr, tr in next tr (sp over shadow sp made); * 1 shadow sp, 1 bl, (ch 1, tr in next tr) twice (shadow sp over shadow sp made); make 2 more shadow sps, 1 bl, 1 shadow sp, 3 sps. Repeat from * once more; 1 shadow sp, 1 bl, 3 shadow sps, 1 bl, 1 shadow sp, 2 sps, 1 bl, 3 shadow sps, 1 bl, (1 shadow sp, 3 sps, 1 shadow sp, 1 bl, 3 shadow sps, 1 bl) twice; 1 shadow sp, 1 sp, 1 shadow sp, 4 bls. Ch 4, turn. **4th row:** 4 bls, 1 shadow sp, ch 3, tr in next tr (sp over sp made); make 1 more sp, 1 shadow sp, 3 bls, 1 shadow sp, (5 sps, 1 shadow sp, 3 bls, 1 shadow sp) twice; 4 sps, 1 shadow sp, 3 bls, 1 shadow sp, (5 sps, 1 shadow sp, 3 bls, 1 shadow sp) twice; 2 sps, 1 shadow sp, 4 bls. Ch 4, turn. Starting with the 5th row, follow chart to top. Fasten off.

Make 5 x 6 squares and sew together on wrong side with neat over-and-over sts. Block to measurements given.

There are 10 spaces between heavy lines

◀— START HERE —▶

□ — SP.   ⊡ — SHADOW SP.   ■ — BL.

WEDGWOOD DOILY

CLASSIC DISTINCTION MARKS THIS FAVORED ROSE DESIGN LACE DOILY

MATERIALS:

J. & P. COATS or CLARK'S O.N.T. BEST SIX CORD MERCERIZED CROCHET, size 30:

SMALL BALL:
J. & P. COATS —2 balls of White or Ecru, or 3 balls of any color,

OR

CLARK'S O.N.T.—4 balls of White, Ecru or any color.

BIG BALL:
J. & P. COATS —1 ball of White or Ecru.

Steel Crochet Hook No. 10 or 11.

Doily measures 16 inches in diameter.

GAUGE: 4 sps make 1 inch; 4 rows make 1 inch.

Starting at bottom of chart, ch 67.
1st row: Tr in 11th ch from hook, * ch 3, skip 3 ch, tr in next ch. Repeat from * across (15 sps). Ch 18, turn.
2nd row: Tr in 11th ch from hook, ch 3, skip 3 ch, tr in next ch, ch 3, skip 3 ch, tr in next tr (3 sps increased); (ch 3, tr in next tr) 14 times; ch 3, skip 3 ch, tr in next ch, ch 7, tr in same place as last tr (1 sp increased); (turn, ch 7, skip 3 sts of 1st ch-7, tr in next ch) twice (2 more sps increased); sl st across last 3 ch. Ch 18, turn. **3rd row:** Tr in 11th ch from hook, ch 3, skip 3 ch, tr in next ch, ch 3, skip 3 ch, tr in next tr, ch 3, skip 3 ch, tr in same place as last sl st, ch 3, tr in top of next tr, ch 3, tr in base of same tr, (ch 3, tr in next tr) 18 times; ch 3, skip 3 ch, tr in next ch, ch 7, tr in same place as last tr, (turn, ch 7, skip 3 sts of 1st ch-7, tr in next ch) twice (3 sps increased at each end); sl st across last 3 ch. Ch 14, turn. **4th row:** Inc 2 sps as before, make 7 more sps, 3 tr in next sp, tr in next tr (bl over sp made), make 12 more bls, 11 sps. Ch 14, turn. **5th row:** 8 sps, 3 bls, tr in next 4 tr (bl over bl made); make 15 more bls, 8 sps. Ch 10, turn.

Starting with 6th row, follow chart until 14th row is completed. Ch 10, turn. **15th row:** 4 sps, 3 bls, 11 sps, 3 bls, 2 sps, 3 bls, 3 sps, 1 bl, 1 sp, ch 1, skip 1 ch, tr in next ch, ch 1, tr in next tr (1 shadow sp made); make 2 more shadow sps, 1 sp, 1 bl, 3 shadow sps, 8 sps, 3 bls, 4 sps. Ch 10, turn. **16th row:** 4 sps, 3 bls, 8 sps, 1 shadow bl, (ch 1, tr in next tr) twice (shadow bl over shadow bl made); make 3 more shadow bls, 1 sp, 5 shadow bls, 4 sps, 3 bls, 1 sp, 6 bls, 10 sps, 3 bls, 4 sps. Ch 7, turn. Starting with 17th row, follow chart until 40th row is complete. Do not ch to turn. **41st row:** Sl st across to 1st tr (1 sp decreased), ch 7, follow chart across row to within last sp, do not work over this sp. Ch 7, turn. Now follow chart to top. Do not fasten off, but work a row of sc closely around edge, keeping work flat. Join and fasten off.

Starch lightly if desired and block to measurement given.

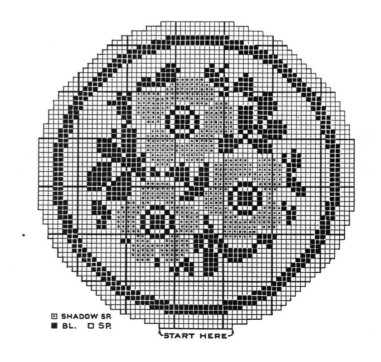

☐ SHADOW SP.
■ BL. ☐ SP.

START HERE

FILET FLOWER PILLOW

Pillow measures 14 x 20 inches.

GAUGE: 4½ sps make 1 inch; 4½ rows make 1 inch.

Starting at one long end, make a chain about 24 inches long. **1st row:** Dc in 8th ch from hook, * ch 2, skip 2 ch, dc in next ch (2 sps made). Repeat from * across until there are 88 sps. Ch 5, turn. Cut off remaining chain. **2nd row:** Dc in next dc, * ch 2, dc in next dc. Repeat from * across, ending with ch 2, skip 2 sts of turning ch, dc in next ch (sps made over sps). Ch 5, turn. **3rd row:** Dc in next dc, ch 2, dc in next dc, 2 dc in next sp, dc in next dc (bl made over sp). Work (1 sp, 2 bls, 4 sps, 3 bls) 7 times; 1 sp, 2 bls, 4 sps, 1 bl, 1 sp, 1 bl, 5 sps. Ch 5, turn. **4th row:** 4 sps, 1 bl, (1 sp, 1 bl) twice; * (2 sps, 1 bl) twice; 3 sps, 1 bl. Repeat from * 6 more times; then work (2 sps, 1 bl) twice and 3 sps. Ch 5, turn. Starting with 5th row, follow chart to top. Fasten off.

FINISHING . . . Pin crocheted piece out to measurements given and press with hot iron through damp cloth. Sew onto pillow.

An enchanting pillow is such a delightful accessory

MATERIALS:

J. & P. COATS or CLARK'S O.N.T. BEST SIX CORD MERCERIZED CROCHET, size 20:

SMALL BALL:
J. & P. COATS —4 balls of White or Ecru,
    OR
CLARK'S O.N.T.—6 Balls of White or Ecru.

BIG BALL:
J. & P. COATS —2 balls of White or Ecru.

Steel Crochet Hook No. 9 or 10.

A pillow 14 x 20 inches.

There are 10 spaces between heavy lines

← **START HERE** →

PEACOCK PARADE CLOTH

A NEW ARABIAN NIGHT'S FANTASY ... MAGNIFICENT PEACOCK CLOTH!

MATERIALS:

J. & P. COATS or **CLARK'S O.N.T. BEST SIX CORD MERCERIZED CROCHET**, size 30:

SMALL BALL:
J. & P. COATS —36 balls of White or Ecru, or 48 balls of any color,

OR

CLARK'S O.N.T.—58 balls of White, Ecru or any color.

BIG BALL:
J. & P. COATS —18 balls of White or Ecru.

Steel Crochet Hook No. 9 or 10.

Tablecloth measures about 72 x 90 inches.

GAUGE: 5 sps make 1 inch; 5 rows make 1 inch.

Starting at bottom of chart, make a chain about 75 inches long (14 ch sts to 1 inch). **1st row:** Dc in 8th ch from hook, ch 2, skip 2 ch, dc in next ch (2 sps made), dc in next 9 ch (3 bls made), (ch 2, skip 2 ch, dc in next ch) 5 times; dc in next 9 ch, (ch 2, skip 2 ch, dc in next ch) twice; dc in next 60 ch (20 bls made), 5 sps, 54 dc (18 bls made), 12 sps, (9 dc, 8 sps) twice; 9 dc, 12 sps, 45 dc (15 bls made), 5 sps, 9 dc, 5 sps, 45 dc, 12 sps, 9 dc, 8 sps, 9 dc, 7 sps, 9 dc, 8 sps, 9 dc, 12 sps, 45 dc, 5 sps, 9 dc, 5 sps, 45 dc, 12 sps, 9 dc, (8 sps, 9 dc) twice; 12 sps, 54 dc, 5 sps, 60 dc, 2 sps, 9 dc, 5 sps, 9 dc, 2 sps. Cut off remaining chain. Ch 5, turn. **2nd row:** Dc in next dc (sp over sp made), 2 dc in next sp, dc in next dc (bl over sp made), (ch 2, skip 2 dc, dc in next dc) 3 times (3 sps over 3 bls made); 2 bls, ch 2, dc in next dc (sp over sp made), 2 bls, 3 sps, 2 bls, 1 sp, dc in next 3 dc (bl over bl made), (1 sp, 1 bl) 5 times; 8 sps, 5 bls, 4 sps, (1 bl, 1 sp) 6 times; 3 bls, 9 sps, (2 bls, 3 sps, 2 bls, 4 sps) twice; 2 bls, 3 sps, 2 bls, 9 sps, 3 bls, (1 sp, 1 bl) twice; 9 sps, 2 bls, 2 sps, 5 bls, 2 sps, 2 bls, 9 sps, (1 bl, 1 sp) twice; 3 bls, 9 sps, 2 bls, 3 sps, 2 bls, 4 sps, (2 bls, 3 sps) 3 times; 2 bls, 4 sps, 2 bls, 3 sps, 2 bls, 9 sps, 3 bls, (1 sp, 1 bl) twice; 9 sps, 2 bls, 2 sps, 5 bls, 2 sps, 2 bls, 9 sps, (1 bl, 1 sp) twice; 3 bls, 9 sps, (2 bls, 3 sps, 2 bls, 4 sps) twice; 2 bls, 3 sps, 2 bls, 9 sps, 3 bls, (1 sp, 1 bl) 6 times; 4 sps, 5 bls, 8 sps, (1 bl, 1 sp) 6 times; 2 bls, 3 sps, 2 bls, 1 sp, 2 bls, 3 sps, 1 bl, ch 2, skip 2 ch, dc in next ch. Ch 3, turn.

Note: Chart shows one quarter of design. To make other half of each row, omit center sp or bl, as the case may be, and work back to the beginning.

Starting with 3rd row, follow chart to top, omit last row, then reverse chart and work back to 1st row. Fasten off.

EDGING ... Ch 14. **1st row:** Dc in 8th ch from hook, (ch 2, skip 2 ch, dc in next ch) twice. Ch 5, turn. **2nd row:** Dc in next dc, ch 2, in next dc make dc, ch 2 and dc; ch 2, dc in 3rd st of turning ch. Ch 5, turn. **3rd row:** Dc in next dc, 2 dc in sp, dc in next dc, ch 2, dc in next dc, 2 dc in sp, dc in 3rd st of turning ch. Ch 3, turn. **4th row:** Dc in 3 dc, ch 2, dc in 3 dc, in next dc make dc, ch 2 and dc; ch 2, dc in 3rd st of turning ch. Ch 5, turn. **5th row:** Dc in next dc, ch 2, dc in 4 dc, ch 2, dc in 3 dc, dc in top st of turning ch. Ch 3, turn. **6th row:** Dc in 3 dc, ch 2, dc in 4 dc, ch 2, in next dc make dc, ch 2 and dc; ch 2, dc in top st of turning ch. Ch 5, turn. **7th row:** Dc in next dc, (ch 2, dc in next dc) twice; dc in next 3 dc, ch 2, dc in next 3 dc, dc in top st of turning ch. Ch 3, turn. **8th row:** Dc in 3 dc, 2 dc in sp, dc in 4 dc, 2 dc in sp, dc in dc, 2 dc in sp, in next dc make dc, ch 2 and dc; ch 2, dc in 3rd st of turning ch. Ch 5, turn. **9th row:** Dc in next dc, ch 2, dc in next dc, ch 2, skip 2 dc, dc in next dc. Ch 5, turn. The 2nd to 9th rows constitute pattern. Repeat pattern until piece is long enough to go around edge of cloth, matching sp for sp and allowing enough at corners to keep flat.

Sew edging to cloth. Block to measurement.

DISPLAY YOUR CROCHET SKILL WITH THIS SUMPTUOUS "WORK OF ART"

FILET LUNCHEON SET

ROYAL SOCIETY SIX CORD CORDICHET, Small Ball, Size 50: 10 balls of White only.
Steel Crochet Hook No. 14.
Runner measures 11 x 30 inches; each Place Mat 11 x 17 inches.

GAUGE: 6 sps measure 1 inch; 6 rows measure 1 inch.

RUNNER . . . Starting at short end, make a chain 12 inches long (18 ch sts to 1 inch). **1st row:** Dc in 4th ch from hook and in the next 62 dc (21 bls); (ch 2, skip 2 ch, dc in next ch) 21 times (21 sps); dc in next 64 dc (21 bls). Cut off remaining chain. Ch 3, turn. **2nd row:** Dc in next 3 dc (bl made over bl), (ch 2, skip 2 dc, dc in next dc) 7 times (7 sps made over 7 bls); dc in next 15 dc (5 bls made over 5 bls); 7 sps, 1 bl, 21 sps, 1 bl, 7 sps, 5 bls, 7 sps, 1 bl, making last dc in 3rd st of turning ch-3. Ch 3, turn. **3rd row:** 1 bl, ch 2, dc in next dc (sp made over sp), 2 dc in next sp, dc in next dc (bl made over sp), 6 sps, 3 bls, 6 sps, 1 bl, 1 sp, 1 bl, 21 sps, 1 bl, 1 sp, 1 bl, 6 sps, 3 bls, 6 sps, 1 bl, 1 sp, 1 bl. Ch 3, turn. **4th to 21st rows incl:** Starting with the 4th row, follow chart across, then make 21 sps, follow chart across once more. At end of 21st row, ch 5, turn. **22nd row:** 21 sps, 21 bls, 21 sps. Ch 5, turn. **23rd row:** 21 sps, 1 bl, 7 sps, 5 bls, 7 sps, 1 bl, 21 sps. Ch 5, turn. **24th to 42nd rows incl:** Work 21 sps, then follow chart across, work 21 more sps. Ch 5, turn. At end of 42nd row, ch 3, turn.

Repeat the 1st to 42nd rows incl 3 more times, then repeat the 1st to 21st rows incl once more.

EDGING . . . 1st rnd: Ch 5, working across long side, * make dc in edge of next row, ch 2. Repeat from * across to next corner, ch 2, in corner st make dc, ch 5 and dc. ** Ch 2, skip 2 sts, dc in next st. Repeat from ** across to next corner. Work other two sides to correspond, ending with ch 5, sl st in 3rd st of ch-5. **2nd rnd:** Ch 3, * 2 dc in next sp, dc in next dc. Repeat from * around, making 9 dc in each corner sp. Sl st in top st of ch-3. Break off.

PLACE MAT (Make 2) . . . Make a chain 18 inches long (18 ch sts to 1 inch). **1st row:** (21 bls, 21 sps) twice; 21 bls. Ch 3, turn. **2nd row:** (1 bl, 7 sps, 5 bls, 7 sps, 1 bl, 21 sps) twice; 1 bl, 7 sps, 5 bls, 7 sps, 1 bl. Ch 3, turn. **3rd to 21st rows incl:** (Follow chart across, then make 21 sps) twice; follow chart once more. At end of 21st row, ch 5, turn. **22nd to 42nd rows incl:** (21 sps, follow chart across) twice; 21 sps. Ch 5, turn. At end of 42nd row, ch 3, turn. Repeat the first 21 rows once more. Complete as for Runner.

11

MAIN LINE TABLECLOTH

SIMPLE ELEGANCE IN A STUNNING CLOTH

What You Need:

ROYAL SOCIETY SIX CORD CORDICHET

Small Ball, size 30:

77 balls.

OR

Large Ball, size 30:

24 balls.

Steel Crochet Hook No. 10.

CLOTH 72 INCHES IN DIAMETER

Tablecloth measures about 72 inches in diameter.

GAUGE: 5 sps make 1 inch; 5 rows make 1 inch.

Starting at bottom of chart, ch 39. **1st row:** Dc in 4th ch from hook, dc in 35 ch (12 bls made). Ch 5, turn. **2nd row:** Dc in 4th ch from hook, dc in next ch, dc in 4 dc (bl over bl made), ch 2, sk 2 dc, dc in next dc (sp over bl made), dc in 3 dc, ch 2, sk 2 dc, dc in next dc, dc in 12 dc (4 bls made), 1 sp, 1 bl, 1 sp, dc in 2 dc, then make a foundation dc in top of turning ch as follows: Thread over, insert hook in top of turning ch and pull a loop through; thread over and draw through 1 loop on hook—*ch st made to be used as a foundation st for next dc;* (thread over and draw through 2 loops) twice—*foundation dc completed.* Make 2 more foundation dc and 1 dc in usual way (1 bl increased at both ends of row). Ch 5, turn. **3rd row:** Dc in 4th ch from hook, dc in next ch, 1 bl, 1 sp, 2 dc in next sp, dc in next dc (bl over sp), 1 sp, 1 bl, 1 sp, 2 bls, (1 sp, 1 bl) twice; 1 sp, dc in 2 dc, foundation dc in top st of turning ch, 2 more foundation dc and 1 dc in usual way (1 bl increased at both ends of row). Ch 5, turn.

4th and 5th rows: Follow chart. At end of 5th row, ch 117, turn. **6th row:** Dc in 4th ch from hook, dc in 113 ch (38 bls increased), (1 bl, 1 sp) 4 times; 4 bls, (1 sp, 1 bl) 3 times; 1 sp, dc in 2 dc, foundation dc in top st of turning ch, 114 more foundation dc and 1 dc in usual way (38 bls increased). Ch 8, turn. Starting with the 7th row, follow chart to top. Chart shows one quarter of design. To make second half of each row, repeat first half, starting from center and working back. When work reaches top row, reverse chart and work back to the 1st row. Fasten off.

There are 10 spaces between heavy lines

STEPPING STONES BEDSPREAD

MATERIALS...*J. & P. Coats Bedspread Cotton, 31 balls of White, or 23 balls of Ecru for double size spread; 26 balls of White, or 19 balls of Ecru for single size spread.* Milward's steel crochet hook No. 8 or 9.

GAUGE: Each block measures about 8½ inches square. For a double size spread, 94 x 111 inches, make 71 filet blocks and 72 wheel blocks. For a single size spread, 77 x 111 inches, make 58 filet blocks and 59 wheel blocks.

FILET BLOCK. GAUGE: 4 sps make 1 inch; 4 rows make 1 inch. Starting at bottom, ch 108. **1st row:** D c in 8th ch from hook, * ch 2, skip 2 ch, d c in next ch. Repeat from * across (34 sps). Ch 5, turn. **2nd row:** Skip 2 ch, d c in next d c, ch 2, skip 2 ch, d c in next d c, 2 d c in next sp, d c in next d c (2 sps and 1 bl made). Make 1 more bl, 1 sp, 6 bls, 2 sps, 8 bls, 2 sps, 6 bls, 1 sp, 2 bls, 2 sps. Ch 5, turn. **3rd row:** 1 sp, 2 bls, 2 sps. Hereafter follow chart until block is completed. Fasten and break off.

WHEEL BLOCK...(Four wheels constitute 1 block.) GAUGE: Each wheel measures about 4 inches in diameter.

FIRST WHEEL... Beginning at center, ch 16, join with sl st to form ring. **1st row:** Ch 25, s c in 2nd ch from hook, and in each ch across (24 s c). Make 1 s c in ring. Ch 1, turn. **2nd row:** Picking up only the back loop of each s c, skip 1st s c, s c in each of next 24 s c. Ch 1, turn. **3rd row:** Picking up only the back loop of each s c, s c in each of next 4 s c, * ch 5, s c in each of next 4 s c. Repeat from * across, ending with 4 s c (5 p's made): Make 1 s c in ring. This completes the first spoke. Do not break off but continue for the second spoke.

SECOND SPOKE...1st row: Ch 24, drop loop from hook, insert hook in 3rd p from ring and draw

dropped loop through; s c in each ch of ch-24 (24 s c). Make 1 s c in ring. Ch 1, turn. Repeat the 2nd and 3rd rows of first spoke once. Then make 6 more spokes same as second spoke (8 in all) but, while making the 3rd p of the last spoke, attach to 1st spoke by making ch 2, sl st in end s c of 1st spoke, ch 2, and continue back on 8th spoke as usual. Fasten and break off. This completes one wheel. Make 3 more wheels same as this.

Place wheels in position to form a block (see stitch detail), and sew together on wrong side with neat over-and-over stitches, joining 4 points of each wheel, at each of 2 sides, to 4 points of adjacent wheel. Fill in space between wheels as follows:

FILL-IN LACE... Attach thread to any p at center, and ch 5 (to count as tr and ch-1); * tr in turning ch at tip of next spoke, ch 1, tr in p of next spoke, ch 1. Repeat from * around. Join last ch-1 with sl st to 4th st of ch-5 first made. Fasten and break off.

EDGING...1st rnd: With right side of wheels toward you, attach thread to 2nd free p of 2nd free spoke, counting to the right from joining; * ch 6, s c in turning ch at tip of next spoke, ch 4, s c in next p, ch 4, d c in next p, ch 6, tr tr in turning ch at tip of next spoke, tr tr in 1st free p of next spoke, ch 6, d c in turning ch at tip of next spoke, ch 4, s c in next p, ch 4, s c in following p, ch 6, s c in turning ch at tip of next spoke, ch 4, s c in next p, ch 4, d c in next p, ch 9, tr tr in same place as last d c, tr tr in turning ch at tip of next spoke (this is corner), ch 9, d c in next p, ch 4, s c in next p. Repeat from * around. Join with sl st. **2nd rnd:** Ch 1, * 7 s c in next sp, s c in next s c, 4 s c in next sp, s c in next s c, 4 s c in next sp, s c in next d c, 7 s c in next sp, s c in next tr tr, s c in following tr tr, 7 s c in next sp, s c in d c, 4 s c in next sp, s c in next s c, 4 s c in next sp, s c in next s c, 7 s c in next sp, s c in next s c, 4 s c in next sp, s c in next s c, 4 s c in next sp, s c in d c, 10 s c in next sp, s c in tr tr, ch 3, s c in next tr tr, 10 s c in next sp, s c in d c, 4 s c in next sp, s c in next s c. Repeat from * around. Join with sl st to ch-1 first made. **3rd rnd:** Ch 5 (to count as d c and ch-2); * skip 2 s c, d c in next s c, ch 2. Repeat from * around, working corners as follows: ch 2, d c in corner ch-3, ch 5, d c in same ch-3, ch 2, d c in next s c (32 sps on each side, excluding corner sps). Fasten and break off. This completes wheel block.

Make necessary number of filet blocks and wheel blocks, and sew together neatly on wrong side, alternating blocks, as in illustration, and having wheel blocks at corners (for double size spread, 11 x 13 blocks; for single size spread, 9 x 13 blocks).

Take a filet square, and a square made up of four circles as the ingredients, stir them together in checkerboard effect, and you'll concoct a spread of real individuality and richness.

FILET TRAY MAT

ROYAL SOCIETY SIX CORD CORDICHET,
Small Ball, Size 50: 3 balls of White only.
Steel Crochet Hook No. 14.
⅓ yard of white linen.
Tray Cover measures 13 x 18 inches.

GAUGE: 6 sps measure 1 inch; 6 rows measure 1 inch.

Starting at bottom of chart, make a chain 15 inches long (18 ch sts to 1 inch). **1st row:** Dc in 8th ch from hook, * ch 2, skip 2 ch, dc in next ch. Repeat from * across until there are 77 sps. Cut off remaining chain. Ch 5, turn. **2nd row:** Dc in next dc (sp made over sp), ch 2, dc in next dc (another sp made over sp); (2 dc in next sp, dc in next dc—bl made over sp) 3 times; 21 sps, 4 bls, 17 sps, 4 bls, 21 sps, 3 bls, 2 sps. Ch 5, turn. **3rd row:** 2 sps, dc in next 9 dc (3 bls made over 3 bls); 1 more bl, 18 sps, 2 bls, (ch 2, skip 2 dc, dc in next dc—sp made over bl) twice; 1 bl, 1 sp, 2 bls, 13 sps, 2 bls, 1 sp, 1 bl, 2 sps, 2 bls, 18 sps, 4 bls, 2 sps. Ch 5, turn. Follow chart from the 4th row until 21 rows are complete. **22nd row:** 3 sps, 4 bls, (1 sp, 5 bls) twice; 2 sps. Ch 5, turn. Starting at the 23rd row follow chart to the 64th row incl. Now complete this side by working from the 44th row back to the 22nd row incl. Break off. Attach thread to opposite side and work to correspond. Ch 105 at end of last row. Break off: Sew end of ch-105 to inner edge of first side. Complete other end by working the 21st to 1st rows incl. Work a row of sc around all edges, keeping work flat. Join and break off. Sew lace to linen.

WALTZ TIME DOILY
ROMANTIC BEAUTY IN TRADITIONAL FILET

What You Need:

ROYAL SOCIETY SIX CORD CORDICHET

Small Ball, size 30: 4 balls.

OR

Large Ball, size 30: 1 ball.

Steel Crochet Hook No. 11.

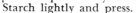

Doily measures about 13 inches in diameter.

GAUGE: 5 sps make 1 inch; 5 rows make 1 inch.

Starting at bottom of chart, ch 42. **1st row:** Dc in 4th ch from hook, dc in 38 ch (13 bls). Ch 8, turn. **2nd row:** Dc in 4th ch from hook, dc in 4 ch, dc in next dc (2 bls increased), ch 2, sk 2 dc, dc in next dc (sp over bl made), make 11 more sps, ch 2, then make a foundation dc as follows: Thread over, insert hook in top st of turning ch and draw a loop through; thread over and draw through 1 loop—*1 ch st made, to be used as a foundation st for next dc;* complete dc in usual manner. Make 5 more foundation dc and 1 dc in the usual way (2 bls increased). Ch 5, turn. **3rd row:** Dc in 4th ch from hook, dc in next ch, dc in next dc, make 2 sps over 2 bls, ch 2, dc in next dc (sp over and draw through 1 loop—*1 ch st made, to be in next dc (bl over sp made), 7 sps, ch 2, foundation dc in top st of turning ch, make 2 more foundation dc and 1 dc in usual way (1 bl increased at both ends). Ch 5, turn. **4th row:** Increase 1 bl, make 8 sps, 1 bl, 1 sp, 1 bl, 8 sps, increase 1 bl. Ch 5, turn. Starting with 5th row, follow chart until 39th row is complete. Do not ch to turn at end of 39th row. **40th row:** Sl st in next 3 dc, ch 3 and follow chart to within last bl (1 bl decreased at both ends). Now follow chart to top to complete doily. Fasten off.

Starch lightly and press.

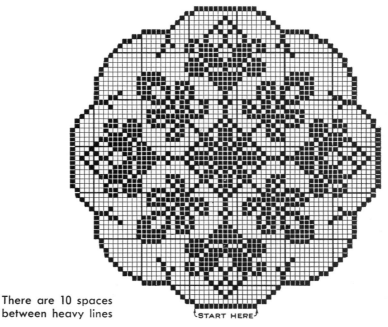

There are 10 spaces
between heavy lines

START HERE

ARISTOCRAT TABLECLOTH

FOR CONNOISSEURS . . . USEFUL SIZE CLOTH . . . ELABORATELY DETAILED

Luncheon cloth measures about 52 in. square.

MATERIALS:

J. & P. COATS or CLARK'S O.N.T. BEST SIX CORD MERCERIZED CROCHET, size 20:

SMALL BALL:

J. & P. COATS —29 balls of White or Ecru,

OR

CLARK'S O.N.T.—50 balls of White or Ecru.

BIG BALL:

J. & P. COATS —17 balls of White or Ecru.

Steel Crochet Hook No. 8 or 9.

Make a chain about 2 yards long (13 ch sts to 1 inch). **1st row:** Dc in 8th ch from hook, * ch 2, skip 2 ch, dc in next ch (sp). Repeat from * until there are 233 sps in all. Ch 5, turn. **2nd row:** Dc in next dc, ch 2, dc in next dc (sp over sp), make 28 more sps, 2 dc in next sp, dc in next dc (bl over sp), make 3 more bls, 6 sps, 3 bls, 6 sps, 4 bls, 27 sps, 4 bls, 6 sps, 3 bls, 6 sps, 4 bls, 27 sps, 4 bls, 6 sps, 3 bls, 6 sps, 4 bls, 27 sps, 4 bls, 6 sps, 3 bls, 6 sps, 4 bls, 29 sps, ch 2, skip 3 sts of turning ch, dc in next ch. Ch 5, turn. **3rd row:** 29 sps, 1 bl, dc in 3 dc (bl over bl made), make 4 more bls, 4 sps, 2 bls, ch 2, skip 2 dc, dc in next

dc (sp over bl made), 2 bls, 4 sps, 6 bls, 25 sps, 6 bls, 4 sps, 2 bls, 1 sp, 2 bls, 4 sps, 6 bls, 25 sps, 6 bls, 4 sps, 2 bls, 1 sp, 2 bls, 4 sps, 6 bls, 25 sps, 6 bls, 4 sps, 2 bls, 1 sp, 2 bls, 4 sps, 6 bls, 29 sps. Ch 5, turn.

Chart shows one quarter of design. To make second half of each row, repeat the first half, starting from center and working back, but do not repeat the exact center sp or bl as the case may be. Follow chart to top; then reverse design by working back to 1st row, but do not repeat top row of chart. Do not fasten off but work a row of sc all around, keeping work flat. Fasten off.

ARGYLE FILET CLOTH

40 Inches Square

MATERIALS: J. & P. Coats or Clark's O.N.T. Best Six Cord Mercerized Crochet, *Size 30,* **Small Ball:** J. & P. Coats—*25 balls of White or Ecru, or 29 balls of any color,* or Clark's O.N.T.—*37 balls of White or Ecru, or 45 balls of any color.* **Big Ball:** J. & P. Coats—*12 balls of White, Ecru or Cream . . . Steel Crochet Hook No. 10.*

GAUGE: 4 sps make 1 inch; 4 rows make 1 inch.

Make a chain 1¼ yards long (16 ch sts to 1 inch). **1st row:** Tr in 5th ch from hook, tr in each ch across until there are 629 tr in all, counting turning ch-4 as 1 tr. Cut off remaining chain. Ch 4, turn. **2nd and 3rd rows:** Skip 1st tr, tr in each tr across, tr in top of turning chain (629 tr). Ch 4, turn. **4th row:** Skip 1st tr, tr in next 12 tr (3 bls made over 3 bls); * ch 3, skip 3 tr, tr in next tr (sp made over bl). Repeat from * across until there are 151 sps, tr in next 11 tr, tr in top of turning chain (3 bls made over 3 bls). Ch 4, turn. **5th to 8th rows incl:** Make 3 bls, * ch 3, tr in next tr (sp made over sp). Repeat from * across until there are 151 sps, make 3 bls. Ch 4, turn. Now work from chart as follows: **1st row:** Make 3 bls, 4 sps; * ch 1, skip 1 ch, tr in next ch, ch 1, tr in next tr (shadow sp made over sp) ; 4 sps, 3 tr in next sp, tr in next tr (bl made over sp), 4 sps, 1 shadow sp, 1 bl, 4 sps, 1 shadow sp, 4 sps, 1 bl. Repeat from * 5 more times; 1 shadow sp, 4 sps, 1 bl, 4 sps, 1 shadow sp, 4 sps, 3 bls. Ch 4, turn. **2nd row:** 3 bls, 4 sps, * ch 3, skip next tr, tr in next tr (sp made over shadow sp), 1 shadow sp, 2 sps, 3 bls, 2 sps, 1 shadow sp, 2 sps, 1 bl, 2 sps, 1 shadow sp, (ch 1, tr in next tr) twice (shadow sp made over shadow sp) ; make 1 more

20

shadow sp, 2 sps, 1 bl, 1 sp. Repeat from * 5 more times; 1 sp, 1 shadow sp, 2 sps, 3 bls, 2 sps, 1 shadow sp, 5 sps, 3 bls. Ch 4, turn. **3rd, 4th and 5th rows:** Follow chart, keeping border as before, working from "A" to "B" 6 times in all, then from "C" to "D" once. Ch 4, turn. **6th row:** 3 bls, 6 sps, * (tr in next ch, tr in next tr) twice (bl made over shadow sp); (ch 1, skip next tr, tr in next tr) twice (shadow sp made over bl); 3 bls, 1 shadow sp, 1 bl, 4 sps, 1 shadow sp, 1 bl, 3 shadow sps, 1 bl, 1 shadow sp, 4 sps. Repeat from * 5 more times; 1 bl, 1 shadow sp, 3 bls, 1 shadow sp, 1 bl, 6 sps, 3 bls. Ch 4, turn.

Starting with the 7th row, follow chart to top, working from "A" to "B" 6 times in all, then from "C" to "D" once. Then starting with 1st row, repeat entire chart 2 more times. Then repeat 1st to 20th rows incl once more. Work remainder of cloth to correspond with beginning. Break off.

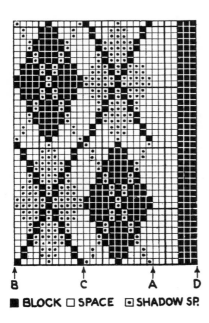

B C A D

■ **BLOCK** □ **SPACE** ▣ **SHADOW SP.**

TEA CLOTH

40 Inches Square   Illustrated on page 22

MATERIALS: J. & P. Coats or Clark's O.N.T. Best Six Cord Mercerized Crochet, Size 30, **Small Ball:** J. & P. Coats—26 balls of White or Ecru, or 32 balls of any color, or Clark's O.N.T.—40 balls of White or Ecru, or 48 balls of any color. **Big Ball:** J. & P. Coats—11 balls of White, Ecru or Cream . . . Steel Crochet Hook No. 10.

GAUGE: 5 sps make 1 inch; 5 rows make 1 inch.

BLOCK . . . Starting at lower edge, make a chain about 10 inches long (15 ch sts to 1 inch). **1st row:** Dc in 8th ch from hook (sp made), ch 2, skip 2 ch, dc in next ch (another sp made), make 39 more sps. Cut off remaining chain. Ch 5, turn. **2nd row:** Dc in next dc (sp made over sp), ch 2, dc in next dc (another sp made over sp), 2 dc in next sp, dc in next dc (bl made over sp), make 6 more bls, 2 sps, 2 bls, 20 sps, 2 bls, 1 sp, 3 bls, 2 sps. Ch 5, turn. **3rd row:** 1 sp, 1 bl, ch 2, skip 2 dc, dc in next dc (sp made over bl), dc in next 3 dc (bl made over bl), 2 more bls, 1 sp, 2 bls, 17 sps, 3 bls, 1 sp, 8 bls, 1 sp, 1 bl, 1 sp. Ch 5, turn. Beginning with the 4th row of chart, follow chart to top. Break off.

Make 5 rows of 5 blocks and sew together on wrong side with neat over-and-over sts, having corresponding parts of design meet (see illustration).

EDGING . . . 1st rnd: Attach thread to corner sp, ch 3, 8 dc in same sp, * dc in next st, 2 dc in next sp. Repeat from * around, making 9 dc in each corner. Join. **2nd rnd:** Ch 3, dc in each dc around. Join and break off.

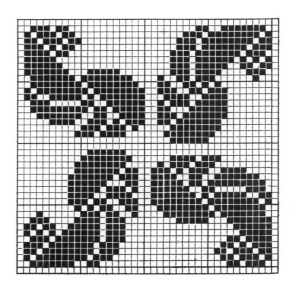

Tea Cloth . . . Directions on page 21

GREENBRIER BEDSPREAD

SIMPLICITY TRIUMPHS IN THE SERENE CLARITY OF THIS FINE PATTERN

MATERIALS:

CLARK'S O.N.T. MERCERIZED BEDSPREAD COTTON, 22 balls of White or Ecru.
Steel Crochet Hook No. 8.

Bedspread (single size only) measures about 74 x 97 inches.

GAUGE: 3 sps (or bls) make 1¼ inches; 3 rows make 1¼ inches. Square measures about 24 x 24 inches.

SQUARE . . . Starting at center, ch 14. Join with sl st to form ring. **1st rnd:** Ch 4 (to count as tr), 4 tr in ring, (ch 7, 5 tr in ring) 3 times; ch 3, tr in 4th st of ch-4. **2nd rnd:** Ch 4, 3 tr in next sp, tr in top st of ch-4 below, tr in next 4 tr, * 4 tr in next sp, ch 7, 4 tr in same sp, tr in next 5 tr. Repeat from * around, ending with ch 3, tr in 4th st of ch-4. **3rd rnd:** Ch 4, 3 tr in next sp, tr in top st of ch-4 below, tr in next 12 tr, * 4 tr in next sp, ch 7, 4 tr in same sp, tr in next 13 tr. Repeat from * around. Join as before. **4th rnd:** Ch 4, 3 tr in next sp, tr in top st of ch-4 below, * (ch 3, skip 3 sts, tr in next tr) twice; tr in next 4 tr, (ch 3, skip 3 sts, tr in next tr) twice; 4 tr in next sp, ch 7, 4 tr in same sp, tr in next tr. Repeat from * around. Join. Starting at 5th rnd (marked with X), follow chart until square is completed, making ch 3 for sps and ch 7 for corner sps and joining each round as before. Fasten off.

Make 3 x 4 blocks and sew them together on wrong side with neat over-and-over sts.

EDGING . . . Attach thread to edge, ch 4 and work 3 rnds of tr, being careful to keep work flat and turning corners same as on squares. Fasten off. Block to measurements given.

PEACOCK BUFFET SCARF

DAISY MERCERIZED CROCHET COTTON, Art. 65: 2¼ skeins White, Size 20; or

LILY MERCERIZED CROCHET COTTON (big balls), Art. 36: 2 balls White, Size 20; or

LILY MERCROCHET MERCERIZED COTTON, Art. 161: 3 balls White, Size 20.

No. 12 Steel Crochet Hook.

Gauge: 5 rows - 1 inch; 5 sps or blks - 1 inch.

Work tightly for best results.

SCARF — (16½ x 26 inches): Ch 250.

Row 1: Starting at A on Chart, sk 4 ch, dc in next 21 ch (7 blks), (ch 2, sk 2 ch, dc in next ch) 5 times (5 sps), continue with 7 blks, 5 sps, (8 blks, 5 sps) 3 times, 7 blks, 5 sps and 7 blks. Mark right side of this row as right side of Scarf.

Row 2: Ch 30, turn, sk 4 ch, dc in next 12 ch, (ch 2, sk 2 ch, dc in next ch) 4 times, dc in next 2 ch, dc in next dc, (4 blks, 4 sps and 1 blk added) continue with 7 blks, 2 dc in next sp, dc in next dc (1 blk), 3 sps, 9 blks and follow Chart across. At end, to add 1 blk, Y O, insert hook in same st where last dc was made, Y O and draw thru 1 lp tightly (a 1-ch), (Y O and draw thru 2 lps) twice to complete dc. * Y O, insert hook in 1-ch made at base of last dc, Y O and draw thru 1 lp (a 1-ch), (Y O and draw thru 2 lps) twice, ** repeat from * once (3 dc

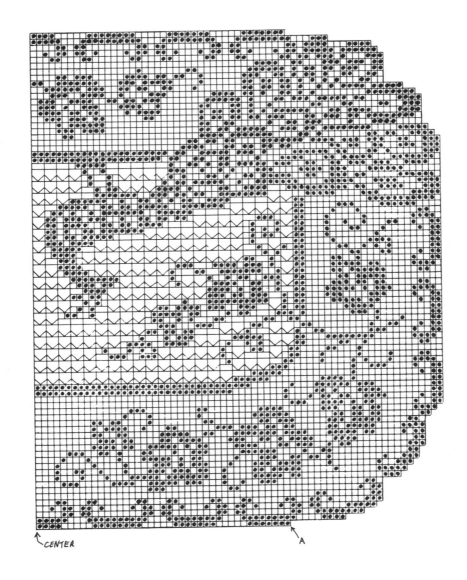

CENTER   A

24

added). Ch 5, dc in 1-ch at base of last dc, (ch 5, turn, dc in 3d st of last ch-5) 3 times (4 added sps); Y O, turn, insert hook in 3d st of last ch-5, Y O and draw thru 1 lp (a 1-ch), (Y O and draw thru 2 lps) twice. Repeat from * to ** 11 times (4 added blks).

Row 3: Ch 12, turn, sk 4 ch, dc in next 8 ch (3 added blks), dc in next dc, 5 blks, 2 sps, 2 blks and follow Chart across, adding 9 dc at end for 3 added blks.

Row 4: Ch 9, turn, sk 4 ch, dc in next 5 ch (2 added blks), dc in next dc, 3 blks, 4 sps, 2 blks, 1 sp and follow Chart across, adding 6 dc at end for 2 added blks.

Row 5: Ch 6, turn, sk 4 ch, dc in next 2 ch (1 added blk), dc in next dc, 2 blks, 5 sps, 1 blk, 1 sp and follow Chart across, adding 3 dc at end for 1 added blk.

Row 6: Working even, ch 3, turn, holding back the last lp of each dc on hook make dc in 1st 2 dc, Y O and draw thru all 3 lps on hook at same time (Cluster-dec), dc in next 5 dc (2 blks), follow Chart across to end.

Row 7: Start as in Row 6.

Row 8: Ch 5, turn, sk 3 dc, dc in next dc (1 sp). Follow Chart across.

Row 9: Start and end as in Row 3.

Rows 10, 11 & 12: Start and end as in Row 5.

Row 13: Start as in Row 6.

Row 14: Start and end as in Row 5.

Rows 15, 16 & 17: Start as in Row 6.

Row 18: Start as in Row 8.

Rows 19, 20 & 21: Start and end as in Row 5. Starting as in Row 6, continue thru Row 24.

Row 25: Ch 3, turn, 2 blks, 12 sps, 1 blk, 1 sp, 4 blks, 8 sps, 6 blks, (ch 3, sk 2 dc, sc in next dc, ch 3, sk 2 dc, dc in next dc) 32 times (32 Lacet Sts), 6 blks and complete row.

Row 26: Ch 3, turn, 2 blks, 1 sp, 1 blk, 10 sps, 1 blk, 11 sps, 5 blks, 1 sp, ch 5, sk 5 dc, dc in next dc, (ch 5, dc in next dc) 32 times, ch 5, sk 5 dc, dc in next dc (34 long sps), 1 sp, 5 blks and complete row.

Row 27: Ch 3, turn, 2 blks, 2 sps, 1 blk, 4 sps, 3 blks, 2 sps, 1 blk, 10 sps, 3 blks, make 2 Lacet Sts, ch 3, sc in next long sp, ch 3, dc in next dc (a 3d Lacet St), ch 5, dc in next dc, 30 Lacet Sts, 1 long sp, 3 Lacet Sts, 3 blks and complete row.

Row 28: Ch 5, turn, sk 3 dc, dc in next dc, 4 blks, (3 sps, 1 blk) twice, 1 sp, (1 blk, 4 sps) twice, 2 blks, 4 long sps, 3 dc in next long sp, ch 2, dc in next dc (1 blk and 1 sp made), complete row as in Chart. Follow Chart thru Row 65.

Next Rows: To decrease at beg. of rows, ch 1, turn, sk 1st dc, sl st in each dc to where next row starts, ch 3 to start next blk or ch 5 to start next sp. Continue thru Row 83. Fasten off.

Stretch and pin right-side-down in true shape. **Steam** and press dry thru a cloth.

ELDORADO DOILY SET

MATERIALS:

CLARK'S O.N.T. or J. & P. COATS BEST SIX CORD MERCERIZED CROCHET
SIZE 50

SMALL BALL:
CLARK'S O.N.T.—*16 balls of White or Ecru or 22 balls of any color,*

OR

J. & P. COATS—*11 balls of White or Ecru or 16 balls of any color.*

BIG BALL:
CLARK'S O.N.T. or J. & P. COATS—*6 balls of White or Ecru.*

Milward's Steel Crochet Hook *No. 12.*

This amount is sufficient for a set consisting of a centerpiece about 14½ inches square; 4 place doilies about 12 inches square; 4 bread and butter plate doilies about 7½ inches square; and 4 glass doilies about 5 inches square.

GAUGE: 6 sps or bls make 1 inch; 6 rows make 1 inch.

CENTERPIECE . . . Starting at bottom of chart, make a chain 18 inches long (17 ch sts to 1 inch). **1st row:**

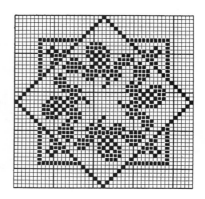

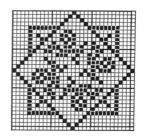

Dc in 8th ch from hook (sp made) * ch 2, skip 2 ch, dc in next ch (another sp made). Repeat from * until there are 42 sps in all, then make dc in next 12 ch (4 bls made). Make 42 sps, then cut off remaining chain. Ch 5, turn. **2nd row:** Dc in next dc, * ch 2, dc in next dc (sp made over sp). Repeat from * until there are 41 sps in all. Make 2 dc in next sp, dc in next dc (bl made over sp); ch 2, skip 2 dc, dc in next dc (sp made over bl). Make 3 more sps, 1 bl, 41 sps. Ch 5, turn. Starting with 3rd row, follow chart to top. Do not fasten off, but work sc completely around, keeping work flat. Fasten off.

PLACE DOILIES (Make 4) . . . Starting at bottom, make a chain 15 inches long (17 ch sts to 1 inch). **1st row:** Dc in 8th ch from hook, * ch 2, skip 2 ch, dc in next ch. Repeat from * until there are 35 sps in all; then make dc in next 6 ch (2 bls made). Make 35 sps, then cut off remaining chain. Ch 5, turn. Starting with 2nd row, follow chart to top. Do not fasten off but work sc completely around, keeping work flat. Fasten off.

BREAD and BUTTER PLATE DOILIES (Make 4) . . . Starting at bottom of chart, chain 140, and follow chart for first row, making 22 sps, 1 bl and 22 sps. Ch 5, turn. Follow chart to top but do not fasten off. Work sc around, keeping work flat. Fasten off.

GLASS DOILIES (Make 4) . . . Starting at bottom of chart, chain 98, and follow chart for 1st row, making 15 sps, 1 bl and 15 sps. Ch 5, turn. Follow chart to top, but do not fasten off. Work sc around, keeping work flat. Fasten off. Block all pieces to measurements.

FILET CORNER TRAY CLOTH

Breakfast in bed becomes a habit with this delightful tray cloth using crocheted corners around fine linen.

MATERIALS... Choose one of the following threads in size 20, White or Ecru:

Clark's O.N.T. Mercerized Crochet, 2 balls.
J. & P. Coats Mercerized Crochet, 1 ball.
J. & P. Coats Big Ball Best Six Cord Mercerized Crochet, 1 ball.

Milward's steel crochet hook No. 8 or 9.
½ yd. linen, 18 inches wide.

GAUGE: 5 sps or bls make 1 inch;
5 rows make 1 inch.

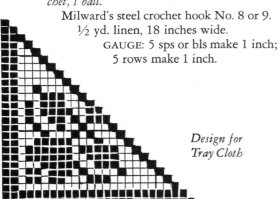

*Design for
Tray Cloth*

FILET CORNER...(Make 4). Starting at bottom of chart, make a chain about 7 inches long. **1st row:** D c in 4th ch from hook, d c in each ch across until 76 d c in all are made (counting turning ch-3 as 1 d c). Cut off remaining chain. Turn. **2nd row:** Sl st in each of 1st 4 d c, ch 3 (to count as d c), d c in each d c across. Ch 3, turn. **3rd row:** D c in each of next 6 d c (2 bls made), * ch 2, skip 2 d c, d c in next d c (1 sp made). Repeat from * across to within 6th d c from end of row (20 sps made), d c in each of last 3 d c (1 bl made). Turn. **4th row:** Sl st in each of 1st 4 d c, ch 3, 2 d c in ch-2 sp, d c in next d c (another bl made), ch 2, d c in next d c; make 6 more sps, 3 bls, 3 sps, 2 bls, 1 sp, 2 bls, 1 sp, 2 bls. Ch 3, turn. Hereafter follow chart, making decreases as before, until corner is completed. Fasten and break off. Cut linen 13 x 18 inches, and make a ¼-inch hem all around, omitting corners. Sew crocheted corners to linen as in illustration. Cut away excess linen, and make a ¼-inch hem at corners.

ROUND ROSE DOILY

Finished about 20" in Diameter

Use Royal Society Cordichet #30 in White or Ecru, 5 balls.

Crochet Hook #9.

M: Mesh.

Start with 15 ch at "A", 1 dc in 9th ch from hook, * ch 2, sk 2 (1 M), 1 dc next ch, repeat from *. Turn, ch 5, 1 dc next dc, 2 M, turn, ch 11, 1 dc in 9th ch from hook, ch 2, 1 dc in next dc (this increases 2 M at start of row) 1 M, 2 dc in M, 1 dc in next dc (1 Bl), 1 M, ch 5, 1 dc in same st as last dc, turn, ch 5, 1 dc in 3rd st of ch 5 following M. (This increases 2 M on end of row.)

To increase 1 M at start of row—ch 8, 1 dc in 1st ch. To increase 1 M at end of row—ch 2, 1 d tr c in same st as last dc.

To increase a number of M at start of row—add 3 ch to 1st 8 ch for each mesh required, 1 dc in 3rd ch from hook, ch 2, sk 2, 1 dc in next ch, etc.

To increase a number of M at end of row—* ch 5, 1 dc in same st as last dc, (1st M) turn, ch 5, 1 dc in 3rd ch, of ch 5 (2nd M), repeat from * as many even M as required, say, 4-6 or 8.

When M required are odd numbers, say, 3-5 or 7, finish last mesh with ch 2, 1 d tr c in same st as last dc. Follow diagram for pattern, spaces indicate meshes (M), crosses indicate blocks (Bl).

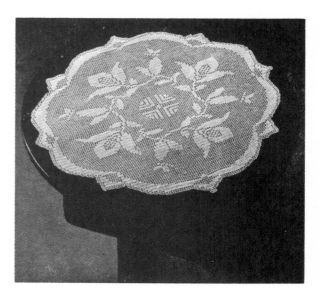

ROSE FILET LUNCHEON SET

ROYAL SOCIETY SIX CORD CORDICHET,
Small Ball, Size 50: 10 balls of White only.
Steel Crochet Hook No. 14.
Each Place Mat measures 11 x 17 inches.

GAUGE: 6 sps measure 1 inch; 6 rows measure 1 inch.

PLACE MAT (Make 3) . . . Starting at bottom, make a chain 20 inches long (18 ch sts to 1 inch). **1st row:** Dc in 8th ch from hook, * ch 2, skip 2 ch, dc in next ch. Repeat from * across until there are 103 sps. Cut off remaining chain. Ch 5, turn. **2nd row:** Dc in next dc (sp made over sp), (2 dc in next sp, dc in next dc —bl made over sp) 3 times; (1 sp, 3 bls, 1 sp, 5 bls) 9 times; (1 sp, 3 bls) twice; ch 2, skip 2 ch, dc in next ch. Ch 5, turn. **3rd row:** 1 sp, dc in next 9 dc (3 bls made over 3 bls), (1 sp, 3 bls, 1 sp, 5 bls) 9 times; (1 sp, 3 bls) twice; 1 sp. Ch 5, turn. **4th row:** 1 sp, 2 bls, ch 2, skip 2 dc,

dc in next dc (sp made over bl), 96 more sps, 2 bls, 1 sp. Ch 5, turn. Follow chart from 5th row to top. Do not break off.

EDGING . . . Make 3 sc in sp, sc at end of next row, ch 3, sl st in last sc—a picot made. Working across short side, make * (2 sc in next sp, sc in next row) 5 times; picot, 2 sc in next sp, sc in next row, picot; (2 sc in next sp, sc in next row) 3 times; picot, 2 sc in next sp, sc in next row, picot. Repeat from * across, ending with a picot, in corner sp make 2 sc, picot and 2 sc; sc in next dc, picot. Work other 3 sides to correspond. Join and break off.

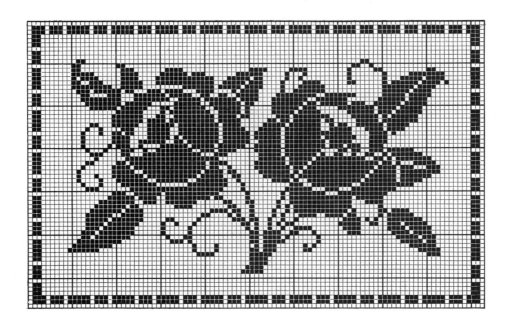

ROUND the CORNER TABLECLOTH

61 x 86 Inches

MATERIALS: J. & P. Coats Knit-Cro-Sheen, *17 balls of White or Ecru . . . Steel Crochet Hook No. 7.*

GAUGE: 3 sps make 1¼ inches; 3 rows make 1¼ inches.

STRIP (Make 7) . . . Make a chain about 12 inches long (10 ch sts to 1 inch). **1st row:** Tr in 5th ch from hook, tr in next 3 ch (bl made), ch 3, skip 3 ch, tr in next ch (sp made), make 2 more sps, tr in next 4 ch (another bl made), 2 sps, 1 bl, 1 sp, 2 bls, 1 sp, 1 bl, 2 sps, 1 bl, 3 sps, 1 bl. Cut off remaining chain. Ch 7, turn. **2nd row:** Skip 4 sts, tr in next tr (sp made over bl), 3 tr in sp, tr in next tr (bl made over sp), make another bl, ch 3, tr in next tr (sp made over sp), tr in next 4 tr (bl made over bl), 2 sps, 1 bl, 1 sp, ch 3, skip 3 tr, tr in next tr (sp made over bl), 2 more sps, 1 bl, 2 sps, 1 bl, 1 sp, 2 bls, 1 sp. Ch 7, turn. Follow chart to top. Repeat entire chart 9 times. Break off.

Sew strips together on wrong side with neat over-and-over sts.

BORDER . . . 1st rnd: Attach thread in corner bl, ch 11, tr in same place where thread was attached, * ch 3, skip 3 sts, tr in next st. Repeat from * across to next corner, in corner make tr, ch 7 and tr. Then work a sp over each row along long side. Work other 2 sides to correspond, making tr, ch 7 and tr at corners. Join to 4th st of ch-11. **2nd rnd:** Ch 4, in corner sp make 4 tr, ch 7 and 4 tr; * tr in next tr, 3 tr in sp. Repeat from * around, making other corners to correspond. Join. **3rd rnd:** Ch 4, tr in each tr around, making 4 tr, ch 7 and 4 tr at corners. Join. Break off.

EAGLE and MOTTO RUNNER GALLANTLY PICTURED IN FINE FILET

What You Need:

ROYAL SOCIETY SIX CORD CORDICHET

Small Ball, size 50: 10 balls.

Steel Crochet Hook No. 12.

GAUGE: 9 sps make 2 inches; 9 rows make 2 inches.

Starting at bottom of chart, make a chain 20 inches long (18 ch sts to an inch). **1st row:** Tr in 5th ch from hook, tr in next 3 ch (1 bl made); * (ch 1, sk 1 ch, tr in next ch) 4 times (2 shadow sps made); (ch 3, sk 3 ch, tr in next ch) twice (2 sps made); tr in next 8 ch. Repeat from * 5 more times; 2 shadow sps, (2 sps, 2 shadow sps, 2 bls) 6 times; 2 sps, 2 shadow sps, 1 bl. Cut off remaining ch. Ch 5, turn. **2nd row:** Sk next tr, tr in next tr, ch 1, sk next tr, tr in next tr (shadow sp over bl made); (ch 1, tr in next tr) 4 times (2 shadow sps over 2 shadow sps made); (ch 3, tr in next tr) twice (2 sps over 2 sps made); * tr in next 8 tr (2 bls over 2 bls made); make 2 shadow sps, 2 sps. Repeat from * 5 more times; 2 shadow sps, (2 bls, 2 sps, 2 shadow sps) 6 times; 1 shadow sp. Ch 5, turn. **3rd row:** 3 shadow sps, (2 sps, 2 bls, 2 shadow sps) 6 times; 2 sps, (2 shadow sps, 2 bls, 2 sps) 6 times; 3 shadow sps. Ch 7, turn. **4th row:** Sk next tr, tr in next tr, (ch 3, sk next tr, tr in next tr) twice (3 sps over 3 shadow sps made); (2 sps, 2 bls, 2 shadow sps) 6 times; 2 sps, (2 shadow sps, 2 bls, 2 sps) 6 times; 3 sps. Ch 7, turn.

5th row: 4 sps, ch 1, tr in sp, ch 1, tr in next tr (shadow sp over sp made); make 71 more shadow sps, 4 sps. Ch 4, turn. **6th row:** (3 tr in next sp, tr in next tr) 4 times (4 bls over 4 sps made); 1 shadow sp, 70 sps, 1 shadow sp, 4 bls. Ch 4, turn. Starting with the 7th row, follow chart until 12th row is completed. Ch 4, turn. **13th row:** 4 bls, 1 shadow sp, 57 sps, 1 bl, ch 3, sk 3 tr, tr in next tr (sp over bl made); 12 sps, 1 shadow sp, 4 bls. Ch 5, turn. Starting with the 14th row, follow chart until 21st row is completed. Ch 7, turn. **22nd row:** 4 sps, 1 shadow sp, 9 sps, 1 shadow sp, 7 sps, 1 bl, 9 sps, 4 shadow sps, 1 sp, (tr in next sp, tr in next tr) 4 times (2 bls over 2 shadow sps made); 2 sps, 2 bls, 1 sp, 4 shadow sps, 17 sps, 1 shadow sp, 9 sps, 1 shadow sp. 4 sps. Ch 7, turn. Starting with the 23rd row, follow chart to top. You have now worked 7 rows of the standard of corresponding design. Reverse chart and, starting with the row marked "X", work back to 1st row to complete design. Fasten off.

Starch lightly and press.

There are 10 spaces between heavy lines

⊡ —SHADOW SP.   ■—BL.   □—SP.

Eagle
and
Motto
Runner

18 X 44 INCHES

Grapevine
Cloth

42 INCHES SQUARE

Directions on page 36

GRAPEVINE CLOTH

Illustrated on page 35

What You Need:

ROYAL SOCIETY SIX CORD CORDICHET

Small Ball, Size 30: 16 balls.

OR

Large Ball, size 30: 5 balls.

Steel Crochet Hook No. 10.

1 yard linen, 36 inches wide.

GAUGE: 5 sps make 1 inch; 5 rows make 1 inch.
Starting at bottom of chart, make a chain about 60 inches long. **1st row:** Dc in 4th ch from hook and in each ch until there are 628 dc (counting turning ch as 1 dc). Cut off remaining ch. Ch 3, turn. **2nd row:** Dc in 9 dc (3 bls over 3 bls made); (ch 2, sk 2 dc, dc in next dc) twice (2 sps over 2 bls made); (6 bls, 16 sps) 4 times; 6 bls, 11 sps, (6 bls, 16 sps) 4 times; 6 bls, 2 sps, 3 bls. Ch 3, turn. **3rd row:** 3 bls, (ch 2, dc in next dc) twice (2 sps over 2 sps made); make 1 more sp, (4 bls, 18 sps) 4 times; 4 bls, 13 sps, (4 bls, 18 sps) 4 times; 4 bls, 3 sps, 3 bls. Ch 3, turn. **4th row:** 1 bl, 86 sps, 2 bls, 31 sps, 2 bls, 86 sps, 1 bl. Ch 3, turn. **5th row:** 1 bl, 29 sps, (2 dc in next sp, dc in next dc) twice (2 bls over 2 sps made); 14 sps, 2 bls, 16 sps, 2 bls, 2 sps, 2 bls, 15 sps, 4 bls, 8 sps, 1 bl, 13 sps, 1 bl, 8 sps, 4 bls, 15 sps, 2 bls, 2 sps, 2 bls, 16 sps, 2 bls, 14 sps, 2 bls, 29 sps, 1 bl. Ch 3, turn.

Note: Chart shows one quarter of entire design and only the first half of each row is shown; to complete each row, omit the center sp or bl, as the case may be, and follow chart back to beginning of row.

Starting with 6th row, follow chart until 30th row is completed. Ch 3, turn. **31st row:** 3 bls, 10 sps, 1 bl, 1 sp, 3 bls, (1 sp, 2 bls) twice; (3 sps, 1 bl) twice; (1 sp, 2 bls) twice; 2 sps, 6 bls, 3 sps, 1 bl. Ch 3, turn. Starting with 32nd row, follow chart until 50th row is completed. Ch 3, turn. **51st row:** 3 bls, 1 sp, 1 bl, 3 sps, 1 bl, 4 sps, 5 bls, (5 sps, 1 bl) twice. Ch 3, turn. Starting with 52nd row, follow chart to top; then reverse chart and, omitting last row, work back to 51st row incl. The end of the 51st row is the inner

edge of piece. Ch 63, turn. **Next row:** Dc in 4th ch from hook and in each ch across (61 dc, counting turning ch as 1 dc), 1 bl, 5 sps, 1 bl, 6 sps, 3 bls, 5 sps, 1 bl, 1 sp, 2 bls, 3 sps, 2 bls. Ch 3, turn. Now follow chart until 31st row is completed. Fasten off. Count 30 bls (or sps, as the case may be) in from opposite side, attach thread to 4th dc of next bl and work to correspond. Join the 2 sides just completed with ch 327. Then follow chart to 1st row, working across chain. Fasten off.

Cut linen to fit in center of lace, allowing for a narrow hem. Hem linen and sew in place.

There are 10 spaces between heavy lines

CENTER
DO NOT REPEAT

START HERE

ROSES in BLOOM CENTERPIECE

Centerpiece measures about 30 inches in diameter.

MATERIALS:

CLARK'S O.N.T. BEST SIX CORD MERCERIZED CROCHET, *Size 30:*

SMALL BALL:

CLARK'S O.N.T.—12 balls of White or Ecru, or

15 balls of any color.

Steel Crochet Hook No. 10 or 11.

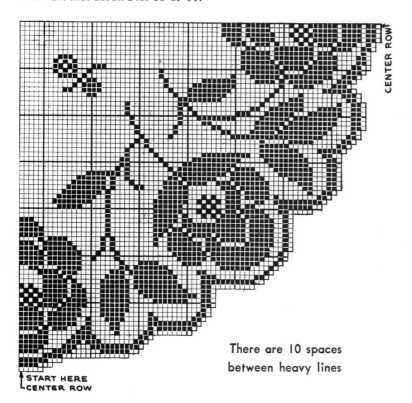

START HERE CENTER ROW

There are 10 spaces between heavy lines

GAUGE: 5 sps measure 1 inch; 5 rows measure 1 inch.

Starting at bottom of chart, ch 32 **1st row:** Dc in 8th ch from hook, (ch 2, skip 2 ch, dc in next ch) 8 times. Ch 10, turn. **2nd row:** Dc in 8th ch from hook, ch 2, dc in next dc (2 sps increased at beginning of row); ch 2, dc in next dc (sp over sp made); (2 dc in next sp, dc in next dc) 7 times (7 bls over 7 sps made); ch 2, skip 2 sts of turning chain, dc in next ch, ch 5, dc in same place as last dc; ch 5, turn, dc in 3rd st of previous ch-5 (2 sps increased at end of row). Ch 10, turn. **3rd row:** Dc in 8th ch from hook, ch 2, dc in top of next dc, ch 2, dc in base of same dc, make 2 bls, dc in next 21 dc (7 bls over 7 bls made); make 2 bls, ch 2, skip 2 sts of turning chain, dc in next ch, ch 5, dc in same place as last dc; ch 5, turn, dc in 3rd st of previous ch-5 (2 sps increased at each end of row). Ch 46, turn. **4th row:** Dc in 8th ch from hook, (ch 2, skip 2 ch, dc in next ch) 12 times; ch 2, dc in top of next dc, make 4 bls, (ch 2, skip 2 dc, dc in next dc) 9 times (9 sps over 9 bls made); make 3 bls, 2 dc in next sp, dc in 5th st of turning chain, ch 5, dc in same place as last dc; (ch 5, turn, dc in 3rd st of previous ch-5) 13 times (14 sps increased at both ends of row). Ch 10, turn. **5th row:** Inc 2 sps, make 6 bls, 6 sps, 4 bls, 3 sps, 7 bls, 3 sps, 4 bls, 6 sps, 6 bls, inc 2 sps. Ch 7, turn. **6th row:** Dc in top of next dc, make 10 bls, 3 sps, 3 bls, 4 sps, 9 bls, 4 sps, 3 bls, 3 sps, 10 bls, ch 5, dc in same place as last dc; turn, sl st to 3rd st of last ch-5 (1 sp increased at both ends). Ch 7, turn.

Continued on page 41

BRIAR ROSE RUNNER and TABLECLOTH

MATERIALS:

J. & P. COATS or CLARK'S O.N.T. BEST SIX CORD MERCERIZED CROCHET, size 20:

SMALL BALL:
J. & P. COATS —11 balls for Runner, 84 balls for Tablecloth,

OR

CLARK'S O.N.T.—18 balls for Runner, 148 balls for Tablecloth.

BIG BALL:
J. & P. COATS —6 balls for Runner, 49 balls for Tablecloth.

Steel Crochet Hook No. 8 or 9.

Runner measures 18 x 42 inches.
Tablecloth measures about 72 x 107 inches.

GAUGE: 4½ sps make 1 inch; 4½ rows make 1 inch.

CHART FOR RUNNER

CENTER ROW —

RUNNER

Starting at bottom of chart, ch 206. **1st row:** Dc in 8th ch from hook (ch 2, skip 2 ch, dc in next ch) 3 times (4 sps made); * dc in next 15 ch (5 bls made); (ch 2, skip 2 ch, dc in next ch) 13 times (13 sps made). Repeat from * 2 more times; make 5 bls, 4 sps. Ch 10, turn. **2nd row:** Dc in 8th ch from hook, ch 2, dc in next dc (2 sps increased); ch 2, dc in next dc (sp over sp made); * (2 dc in next sp, dc in next dc) 3 times (3 bls over 3 sps made); dc in 15 dc (5 bls over 5 bls made); make 3 more bls, 7 sps. Repeat from * 2 more times; 11 bls, ch 2, skip 2 sts of turning chain below, dc in next ch, ch 5, dc in same place as last dc, ch 5, skip 2 sts of previous ch-5, dc in next ch (2 sps increased). Ch 7, turn. **3rd row:** Dc in top of last dc (1 sp increased); ch 2, dc in base of same dc, * 4 bls, (ch 2, skip 2 dc, dc in next dc) 7 times (7 sps over 7 bls made); 4 bls, 3 sps. Repeat from * 2 more times; 4 bls, 7 sps, 4 bls, ch 2, skip 2 ch, dc in next ch, ch 5, dc in same place, turn, sl st in 3 ch (1 sp increased). Ch 7, do not turn. **4th row:** Dc in same place as last sl st (1 sp increased); make 1 sp, * 2 bls, 13 sps, 2 bls, 1 sp. Repeat from * 2 more times; 2 bls, 13 sps, 2 bls, ch 2, skip 2 ch, dc in next ch, ch 5, dc in same place, turn, sl st in 3 ch (1 sp increased). Ch 7, do not turn.

Starting at 5th row, follow chart until 6th row is completed. Ch 5, turn. **7th row:** Dc in next dc, 2 bls, 73 sps, 2 bls, 1 sp. Ch 7, turn. Now follow chart until the 11th row is complete. Ch 3, turn. **12th row:** 2 dc in next sp, dc in next 4 dc, 8 sps, 1 bl, 16 sps, 1 bl, 1 sp, 6 bls, 2 sps, 7 bls, 26 sps, 1 bl, 8 sps, 2 bls. Ch 3, turn. Starting at 13th row, follow chart to top. You are 5 rows beyond center row of runner, and position of design for second half has been established. Starting at row marked "X," follow chart back until all but last 7 rows are completed. Do not ch to turn. **Next row:** Sl st across 2 ch and 1 dc, ch 5, dc in next dc, follow chart across but do not work over last sp (1 sp decreased at each end). Ch 5, turn. Now follow chart to top. Do not fasten off, but work a row of sc closely around edge, keeping work flat. Join and fasten off.

Starch lightly and block.

Continued on page 41

Made for each other

EXOTIC RAMBLING ROSES GARLAND THIS EXQUISITE ENSEMBLE IDEA!

Briar Rose Runner

18 x 42 inches

Briar Rose Tablecloth

72 x 107 inches

Directions on page 41

CENTER—DO NOT REPEAT

CENTER—DO NOT REPEAT

START HERE

Chart for Briar Rose Tablecloth

BRIAR ROSE

Illustrated on page 39

Matching ideas are smart these days, so ensemble your dining room accessories if you'd be noted for your attention to little things.

TABLECLOTH

First Scallop . . . Ch 44. **1st row:** Dc in 8th ch from hook, ch 2, skip 2 ch, dc in next ch (2 sps made); dc in next 27 ch (9 bls made); (ch 2, skip 2 ch, dc in next ch) twice. Ch 7, turn. **2nd row:** Dc in next dc, (2 dc in next sp, dc in next dc) twice (2 bls over 2 sps made); dc in 27 dc (9 bls over 9 bls made); 2 dc in next sp, dc in next dc, 2 dc in next sp, dc in 5th st of turning chain, ch 5, dc in same place as last dc (1 sp increased at both ends). Turn, sl st in 3 ch, ch 7. **3rd row:** Dc in same place as last sl st, make 3 bls, (ch 2, skip 2 dc, dc in next dc) 4 times (4 sps over 4 bls made); 1 bl, 4 sps, 3 bls, ch 5, dc in same place as last dc (1 sp increased at both ends). Turn, sl st in 3 ch, ch 7. **4th row:** Dc in same place as last sl st, make 2 bls, 2 sps, 9 bls, 2 sps, 2 bls, ch 5, dc in same place as last dc (1 sp increased at both ends). Turn, sl st in 3 ch, ch 13. **5th row:** Dc in 8th ch from hook, ch 2, skip 2 ch, dc in next ch, ch 2, dc in next dc, make (2 bls, 2 sps) twice; 3 bls, (2 sps, 2 bls) twice; ch 5, dc in same place as last dc; (ch 5, turn, dc in 3rd st of previous ch-5) twice (3 sps increased at both ends). Turn, sl st in 3 ch, ch 7. **6th row:** Dc in same place as last sl st, 4 bls, 2 sps, 2 bls, 2 sps, 1 bl, 3 sps, 1 bl, 2 sps, 2 bls, 2 sps, 4 bls, ch 5, dc in same place as last dc (1 sp increased at both ends). Fasten off.

Second Scallop . . . Work exactly as for 1st scallop but do not fasten off at end of 6th row. Turn, sl st in 3 ch, ch 8, join with sl st in 5th st of turning chain on 6th row of 1st scallop. Fasten off.

Third and Fourth Scallops . . . Work exactly as for 1st scallop, joining to previous scallop as 2nd was joined to 1st scallop. Fasten off.

Fifth Scallop . . . Ch 110. **1st row:** Dc in 8th ch from hook, ch 2, skip 2 ch, dc in next ch, dc in 18 ch, (ch 2, skip 2 ch, dc in next ch) twice; dc in 45 ch, (ch 2, skip 2 ch, dc in next ch) twice; dc in 18 ch, (ch 2, skip 2 ch, dc in next ch) twice. Ch 7, turn. **2nd row:** Inc 1 sp, make (9 bls, 4 sps) twice; 9 bls, inc 1 sp. Turn, sl st in 3 ch, ch 7. **3rd row:** Inc 1 sp, make 3 bls, 2 sps, 1 bl, 2 sps, 3 bls, 7 sps, 1 bl, 7 sps, 3 bls, 2 sps, 1 bl, 2 sps, 3 bls, inc 1 sp. Turn, sl st in 3 ch, ch 7. **4th row:** Inc 1 sp, make 2 bls, 2 sps, 5 bls, 2 sps, 2 bls, 5 sps, 3 bls, 5 sps, 2 bls, 2 sps, 5 bls, 2 sps, 2 bls, inc 1 sp. Turn, sl st in 3 ch, ch 13. **5th row:** Inc 3 sps, make 2 bls, 2 sps, 2 bls, 3 sps, 2 bls, 2 sps, 2 bls, 4 sps, 3 bls, 4 sps, 2 bls, 2 sps, 2 bls, 3 sps, 2 bls, 2 sps, 2 bls, inc 3 sps. Turn, sl st in 3 ch, ch 7. **6th row:** Inc 1 sp, make 4 bls, 2 sps, 2 bls, 5 sps, 2 bls, 2 sps, (1 bl, 1 sp) twice; 1 bl, 3 sps, (1 bl, 1 sp) twice; 1 bl, 2 sps, 2 bls, 5 sps, 2 bls, 2 sps, 4 bls, inc 1 sp. Turn, sl st in 3 ch, ch 8, join with sl st in 5th st of turning chain on 6th row of 4th scallop. Fasten off.

Sixth to Ninth Scallops incl . . . Work exactly as for 1st scallop, joining to previous scallop as 2nd was joined to 1st scallop. Fasten off.

Attach thread in 3rd st of last increased sp on 1st scallop, ch 7, turn. **7th row:** Dc in same place where thread was attached, * 5 bls, 1 sp, 2 bls, 3 sps, (1 bl, 1 sp) twice; 1 bl, 3 sps, 2 bls, 1 sp, 5 bls, work 3 sps over joining chain. Repeat from * 3 more times; 5 bls, 1 sp, 2 bls, 7 sps, 2 bls, 1 sp, 3 bls, (1 sp, 1 bl) 3 times; 1 sp, 3 bls, 1 sp, 2 bls, 7 sps, 2 bls, 1 sp, 5 bls. ** Work 3 sps over joining chain, 5 bls, 1 sp, 2 bls, 3 sps, (1 bl, 1 sp) twice; 1 bl, 3 sps, 2 bls, 1 sp, 5 bls. Repeat from ** 3 more times; inc 1 sp. Turn, sl st in 3 ch, ch 7.

Note: Chart shows one quarter of design. To make second half of each row, omit center bl or sp as the case may be and work back to beginning of each row.

Starting with the 8th row, follow chart until the 37th row is completed. When there are no increased sps at ends of row, ch 5 to turn. When row begins with a bl, ch 3 to turn. Do not ch to turn at end of 37th row. **38th row:** Sl st in 2 ch, sl st in dc, ch 5, skip 2 dc, dc in next dc, now follow chart across to last sp (1 sp decreased at each end), turn. Now follow chart to the top. The last row on chart is center; to work other half of cloth, reverse chart, omit last row and work back until all but the last 6 rows (scallops) have been completed.

First Scallop . . . 1st row: Dec 1 sp, make 1 sp, 4 bls, 2 sps, 2 bls, 2 sps, 1 bl, 3 sps, 1 bl, 2 sps, 2 bls, 2 sps, 4 bls, 1 sp. Turn. **2nd row:** Dec 1 sp, make 3 sps, (2 bls, 2 sps) twice; 3 bls, (2 sps, 2 bls) twice; 3 sps. Turn. Finish scallop according to chart. Fasten off. * Skip 3 sps, attach thread in next dc, ch 3 and work next scallop across next 27 bls or sps as the case may be. Fasten off. Repeat from * 2 more times. Skip 3 sps, attach thread in next dc, ch 3 and work 5th scallop across next 49 bls or sps. Fasten off. Work remaining 4 scallops to correspond with first 4 scallops. Work a row of sc all around edge. Fasten off.

Block to measurement.

ROSES in BLOOM CENTERPIECE

Continued from page 37

Note: Chart shows one quarter of design. To make second half of each row, omit the center sp or bl, as the case may be, and follow chart back to the beginning of row. Starting with 7th row follow chart to the top. Reverse chart and, omitting last row, follow chart back until the 79th row has been completed. **80th row:** Sl st across 2 ch, sl st in next dc, ch 5 and follow chart across to last sp, do not work over last sp (1 sp decreased at both ends). Ch 5, turn. Now follow chart back to 1st row. Do not fasten off but work sc evenly around edge, keeping work flat. Fasten off. Starch lightly and block to measurement.

FLORAL LUNCHEON SET

6 balls of Royal Society Knitting and Crochet Cotton. Crochet Hook #5.

RUNNER

Foundation ch 115.

1st row: Beginning in 5th ch from hook, work 1 dc in each st of foundation ch, (111 sts).

2nd row: Ch 3, turn. Beginning in 2nd dc, make 1 dc in each of 12 dcs (4 blocks). * ch 2, skip 4 dcs in row below (1 space), make 1 dc in each of 10 dcs (3 bl). Repeat from * 6 times, ch 2, skip 4 dcs in row below (1 sp) and make 1 dc in each remaining st of row. To make a solid sq or block (bl) make 2 dcs between the bars and for the spaces (sp) make ch 2.

3rd row: Ch 3, turn. Beginning in 2nd dc make 1 dc in each of 9 dcs (3 bl). * 3 sp, 1 bl and repeat from * 6 times, then 3 sp, 3 bl.

4th row: Ch 3, turn. Beginning in 2nd dc, make 1 dc in each of 6 dcs (2 bl). Work 33 sp, then 2 bl. The pattern begins in 5th row.

5th row: Ch 3, turn. Beginning in 2nd dc, make 1 dc in each of 3 dcs (1 bl), 6 sp, 2 bl, 3 sp, 1 bl, 4 sp, 2 bl, 5 sp, 1 bl, 3 sp, 2 bl, 6 sp, 1 bl. From this point it will be easy enough to follow the diagram. When center mat is complete, finish the sides and ends with a picot edge, making the picots of ch 5, and placing them according to the pattern with 3 at each corner and filling the spaces between with a close row of sc.

PLATE DOILY

Foundation ch 115.
The plate doily is begun in the same way as the center mat, the only difference being in the length. The edges are finished with 1 row of sc with picots, as indicated in the diagram.
A is the center of the Plate Doily.
B is the center of the Runner.

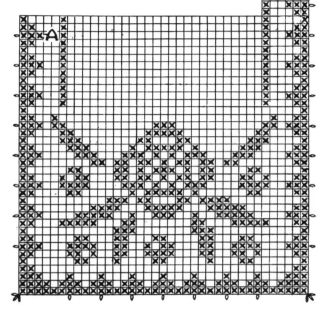

OPEN HOUSE CLOTH

The geometric pattern of this filet cloth has a lovely rhythmic flow that accents its symmetry.

MATERIALS:

J. & P. COATS KNIT-CRO-SHEEN, 31 balls of White or Ecru, or 38 balls of any color.

MILWARD'S Steel Crochet Hook No. 7.

GAUGE . . . 3 sps make 1¼ inches; 3 rows make 1¼ inches. Each block measures about 23½ inches square after blocking. Completed tablecloth measures about 73 x 97 inches.

BLOCK . . . Starting at center, ch 11, tr in 11th ch from hook. Now work in rnds as follows: **1st rnd:** Ch 4, 3 tr over bar of last tr, tr in same ch where first tr of ring was

Continued on page 46

FLORAL CLASSIC TABLECLOTH

MATERIALS... *J. & P. Coats Big Ball Best Six Cord Mercerized Crochet, size 30, 51 balls of White or Ecru.*

Milward's steel crochet hook No. 10.

3 yds. of linen, 18 inches wide, for napkins.

GAUGE: 6 sps make 1 inch; 6 rows of sps make 1 inch.

When completed, tablecloth measures about 73½ x 90 inches excluding the edging, which measures about 4½ inches deep.

Beginning at bottom of chart for tablecloth, make a chain about 3 yds. long. **1st row:** D c in 8th ch from hook, * ch 2, skip 2 ch, d c in next ch (2 sps made). Repeat from * until 440 sps are made. Ch 5, turn. Cut off remainder of foundation chain. **2nd to 13th rows incl:** Skip ch-2, d c in next d c, * ch 2, d c in next d c. Repeat from * across, ending row with ch 2, skip 2 ch, d c in next ch (440 sps). Ch 5, turn. **14th**

Continued on page 46

A classic flower pattern forms the border of this stunning filet banquet cloth.

44

Chart for Tablecloth

There are 10 spaces between heavy lines

FLORAL CLASSIC TABLECLOTH

Continued from page 44

row: Make 35 sps, * 2 d c in next sp, d c in next d c. Repeat from * 2 more times (3 bls made); 6 sps, 2 d c in next sp, d c in next d c (1 bl made); 41 sps, 3 bls, 262 sps, 3 bls, 41 sps, 1 bl, 6 sps, 3 bls, 35 sps. Ch 5, turn. **15th row:** 36 sps, 4 bls, 4 sps, 2 bls, 39 sps, 5 bls, 24 sps, 1 bl, 2 sps, 2 bls, 2 sp, 2 bls, 80 sps, 3 bls, 28 sps, 3 bls, 80 sps, 2 bls, 2 sps, 2 bls, 2 sps, 1 bl, 24 sps, 5 bls, 39 sps, 2 bls, 4 sps, 4 bls, 36 sps. Ch 5, turn. **16th row:** 28 sps, 5 bls, 4 sps, 4 bls, 3 sps, 3 bls, 24 sps, 3 bls, 2 sps, 3 bls, 7 sps, 4 bls, 6 sps, 2 bls, 1 sp, 3 bls, 12 sps, 11 bls, 78 sps, 2 bls, 5 sps, 3 bls, 14 sps, 3 bls, 5 sps, 2 bls, 78 sps, 11 bls, 12 sps, 3 bls, 1 sp, 2 bls, 6 sps, 4 bls, 7 sps, 3 bls, 2 sps, 3 bls, 24 sps, 3 bls, 3 sps, 4 bls, 4 sps, 5 bls, 28 sps. Ch 5, turn. **17th row:** 29 sps, 5 bls, 5 sps, 3 bls, 2 sps, 3 bls, 24 sps, 4 bls, 1 sp, 3 bls, 4 sps, 8 bls, 4 sps, 8 bls, 10 sps, 7 bls, 1 sp, 2 bls, 79 sps, 2 bls, 7 sps, 3 bls, 12 sps, 3 bls, 7 sps, 2 bls, 79 sps, 2 bl, 1 sp, 7 bls, 10 sps, 8 bls, 4 sps, 8 bls, 4 sps, 3 bls, 1 sp, 4 bls, 24 sps, 3 bls, 2 sps, 3 bls, 5 sps, 5 bls, 29 sps. Ch 5, turn. Hereafter follow chart, starting at the 18th row from bottom of chart. Chart shows ¼ of design. To make second half of each row, repeat the first half, starting at center and working back. When work reaches top row, reverse the design by working back from top row to the 1st row.

EDGING... Starting at bottom of chart, ch 84. **1st row:** D c in 4th ch from hook, d c in each of next 2 ch, * ch 2, skip 2 ch, d c in next ch. Repeat from * until 15 sps are made, d c in each of next 3 ch, ch 2, skip 2 ch, d c in next ch; 7 more sps, d c in each of next 3 ch. Ch 5, turn. **2nd row:** D c in 4th ch from hook, d c in next ch, d c in each of next 4 d c (2 bls); 6 sps, 1 bl, 3 sps, 1 bl, 13 sps, 1 bl. Ch 3, turn. **3rd row:** 1 bl, 12 sps, 2 bls, 1 sp, 3 bls, 6 sps, 2 bls. Ch 1, turn. **4th row:** Sl st in each of next 3 d c (1 bl decreased), ch 3, d c in each of next 3 d c, 7 sps, 2 bls, 1 sp, 2 bls, 1 sp, 2 bls, 9 sps, 1 bl. Ch 3, turn. Hereafter follow chart for edging, starting at the 5th row, until design is completed, making scallops at end of chart as follows: Sl st in each of 3 d c, * ch 3 and make 4 bls, turn. Sl st in each of 3 d c, ch 3 and make 2 bls. Fasten and break off. Skip 12 d c, attach thread to next d c. Repeat from * 2 more times. Break off. Attach thread at "X" on chart, and continue to follow chart along other side. This completes one corner. Hereafter work rows of sps (continuing with scallops) until piece is the length of one side, omitting the corner. Then work corner as before, and continue in this manner around. Fasten and break off.

NAPKINS... *(Make 6).* Starting at bottom of chart, ch 78 and follow chart to end. Break off. Cut linen into 6 pieces, 18 inches square. Place lace corner on one corner of linen piece, and sew in place. Cut away excess linen at back of work, and make a narrow hem all around outer edges of napkin. Finish other napkins in same way.

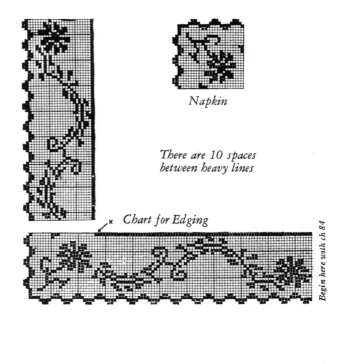

Napkin

There are 10 spaces between heavy lines

Chart for Edging

Begin here with ch 84

OPEN HOUSE CLOTH

Continued from page 43

made, ch 7, tr in same place as last tr, 3 tr in ring, tr in 4th ch of ring, ch 7, tr in same place as last tr, 3 tr in ring (under next 3 ch of ring). Tr in next ch, ch 7, tr in same place as last tr, 3 tr in ring, tr in 1st tr made at base of ch-4. Ch 7, sl st in 4th ch of ch-4 first made. **2nd rnd:** Ch 7, * skip 3 tr, tr in next tr, 3 tr in corner sp. In 4th ch of corner ch-7 make tr, ch 7 and tr; 3 tr in same corner sp, tr in next tr, ch 3. Repeat from * around, ending with 3 tr in corner sp, sl st in 4th ch of ch-7. **3rd rnd:** Ch 7, * tr in next 5 tr, 3 tr in corner sp. In 4th st of corner ch-7 make tr, ch 7 and tr; 3 tr in same corner sp, tr in next 5 tr, ch 3. Repeat from * around; join. **4th rnd:** Ch 7, * tr in next 9 tr (2 bls made); 3 tr in corner sp. In 4th st of corner ch-7 make tr, ch 7 and tr; 3 tr in same corner sp; tr in next 9 tr, ch 3. Repeat from * around; join. Starting at 5th rnd (indicated by "X" on chart), follow chart until block is completed. Fasten off.

Make 3 x 4 blocks, and sew them together on wrong side with neat over-and-over stitches.

EDGING . . . 1st rnd: Attach thread to a tr, ch 4, and work tr in each tr; in the sps make 2 tr and 3 tr, alternately. Work corners same as corners of last rnd of block. Join with sl st. **2nd and 3rd rnds:** Ch 4, tr in each tr around, making corners as for 1st rnd. Fasten off. Block cloth to measurements given.

Simple Crochet Stitches

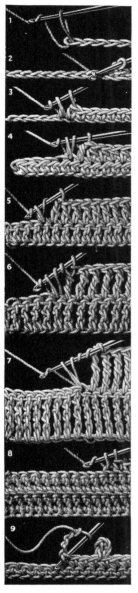

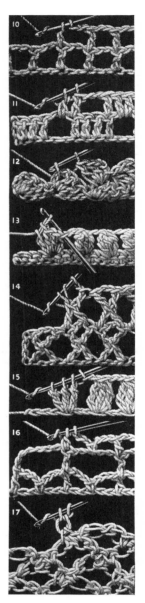

No. 1—Chain Stitch (CH) Form a loop on thread insert hook on loop and pull thread through tightening threads. Thread over hook and pull through last chain made. Continue chains for length desired.

No. 2—Slip Stitch (SL ST) Make a chain the desired length. Skip one chain, * insert hook in next chain, thread over hook and pull through stitch and loop on hook. Repeat from *. This stitch is used in joining and whenever an invisible stitch is required.

No. 3—Single Crochet (S C) Chain for desired length, skip 1 ch, * insert hook in next ch, thread over hook and pull through ch. There are now 2 loops on hook, thread over hook and pull through both loops, repeat from *. For succeeding rows of s c, ch 1, turn insert hook in top of next st taking up both threads and continue same as first row.

No. 4—Short Double Crochet (S D C) Ch for desired length thread over hook, insert hook in 3rd st from hook, draw thread through (3 loops on hook), thread over and draw through all three loops on hook. For succeeding rows, ch 2, turn.

No. 5—Double Crochet (D C) Ch for desired length, thread over hook, insert hook in 4th st from hook, draw thread through (3 loops on hook) thread over hook and pull through 2 loops thread over hook and pull through 2 loops. Succeeding rows, ch 3, turn and work next d c in 2nd d c of previous row. The ch 3 counts as 1 d c.

No. 6—Treble Crochet (TR C) Ch for desired length, thread over hook twice insert hook in 5th ch from hook draw thread through (4 loops on hook) thread over hook pull through 2 loops thread over, pull through 2 loops, thread over, pull through 2 loops. For succeeding rows ch 4, turn and work next tr c in 2nd tr c of previous row. The ch 4 counts as 1 tr c.

No. 7—Double Treble Crochet (D TR C) Ch for desired length thread over hook 3 times insert in 6th ch from hook (5 loops on hook) and work off 2 loops at a time same as tr c. For succeeding rows ch 5 turn and work next d tr c in 2nd d tr c of previous row. The ch 5 counts as 1 d tr c.

No. 8—Rib Stitch. Work this same as single crochet but insert hook in back loop of stitch only. This is sometimes called the slipper stitch.

No. 9—Picot (P) There are two methods of working the picot. (A) Work a single crochet in the foundation, ch 3 or 4 sts depending on the length of picot desired, sl st in top of s c made. (B) Work an s c, ch 3 or 4 for picot and s c in same space. Work as many single crochets between picots as desired.

No. 10—Open or Filet Mesh (O M.) When worked on a chain work the first d c in 8th ch from hook * ch 2, skip 2 sts, 1 d c in next st, repeat from *. Succeeding rows ch 5 to turn, d c in d c, ch 2, d c in next d c, repeat from *.

No. 11—Block or Solid Mesh (S M) Four double crochets form 1 solid mesh and 3 d c are required for each additional solid mesh. Open mesh and solid mesh are used in Filet Crochet.

No. 12—Slanting Shell St. Ch for desired length, work 2 d c in 4th st from hook, skip 3 sts, sl st in next st, * ch 3, 2 d c in same st with sl st, skip 3 sts, sl st in next st. Repeat from *. **2nd Row.** Ch 3, turn 2 d c in sl st, sl st in 3 ch loop of shell in previous row, * ch 3, 2 d c in same space, sl st in next shell, repeat from *.

No. 13—Bean or Pop Corn Stitch. Work 3 d c in same space, drop loop from hook insert hook in first d c made and draw loop through, ch 1 to tighten st.

No. 14—Cross Treble Crochet. Ch for desired length, thread over twice, insert in 5th st from hook, * work off two loops, thread over, skip 2 sts, insert in next st and work off all loops on needle 2 at a time, ch 2, d c in center to complete cross. Thread over twice, insert in next st and repeat from *.

No. 15—Cluster Stitch. Work 3 or 4 tr c in same st always retaining the last loop of each tr c on needle, thread over and pull through all loops on needle.

No. 16—Lacet St. Ch for desired length, work 1 s c in 10th st from hook, ch 3 skip 2 sts, 1 d c in next st, * ch 3, skip 2 sts, 1 s c in next st, ch 3, skip 2 sts 1 d c in next st, repeat from * to end of row, 2nd row, d c in d c, ch 5 d c in next d c.

No. 17—Knot Stitch (Sometimes Called Lovers Knot St.) Ch for desired length, * draw a ¼ inch loop on hook, thread over and pull through ch, s c in single loop of st, draw another ¼ inch loop, s c into loop, skip 4 sts, s c in next st, repeat from *. To turn make ⅜" knots, * s c in loop at right of s c and s c in loop at left of s c of previous row, 2 knot sts and repeat from *.

Metric Conversion Chart

CONVERTING INCHES TO CENTIMETERS AND YARDS TO METERS

mm — millimeters   cm — centimeters   m — meters

INCHES INTO MILLIMETERS AND CENTIMETERS
(Slightly rounded off for convenience)

inches	mm		cm	inches	cm	inches	cm	inches	cm
⅛	3mm			5	12.5	21	53.5	38	96.5
¼	6mm			5½	14	22	56	39	99
⅜	10mm	or	1cm	6	15	23	58.5	40	101.5
½	13mm	or	1.3cm	7	18	24	61	41	104
⅝	15mm	or	1.5cm	8	20.5	25	63.5	42	106.5
¾	20mm	or	2cm	9	23	26	66	43	109
⅞	22mm	or	2.2cm	10	25.5	27	68.5	44	112
1	25mm	or	2.5cm	11	28	28	71	45	114.5
1¼	32mm	or	3.2cm	12	30.5	29	73.5	46	117
1½	38mm	or	3.8cm	13	33	30	76	47	119.5
1¾	45mm	or	4.5cm	14	35.5	31	79	48	122
2	50mm	or	5cm	15	38	32	81.5	49	124.5
2½	65mm	or	6.5cm	16	40.5	33	84	50	127
3	75mm	or	7.5cm	17	43	34	86.5		
3½	90mm	or	9cm	18	46	35	89		
4	100mm	or	10cm	19	48.5	36	91.5		
4½	115mm	or	11.5cm	20	51	37	94		

YARDS TO METERS
(Slightly rounded off for convenience)

yards	meters	yards	meters	yards	meters	yards	meters	yards	meters
⅛	0.15	2⅛	1.95	4⅛	3.80	6⅛	5.60	8⅛	7.45
¼	0.25	2¼	2.10	4¼	3.90	6¼	5.75	8¼	7.55
⅜	0.35	2⅜	2.20	4⅜	4.00	6⅜	5.85	8⅜	7.70
½	0.50	2½	2.30	4½	4.15	6½	5.95	8½	7.80
⅝	0.60	2⅝	2.40	4⅝	4.25	6⅝	6.10	8⅝	7.90
¾	0.70	2¾	2.55	4¾	4.35	6¾	6.20	8¾	8.00
⅞	0.80	2⅞	2.65	4⅞	4.50	6⅞	6.30	8⅞	8.15
1	0.95	3	2.75	5	4.60	7	6.40	9	8.25
1⅛	1.05	3⅛	2.90	5⅛	4.70	7⅛	6.55	9⅛	8.35
1¼	1.15	3¼	3.00	5¼	4.80	7¼	6.65	9¼	8.50
1⅜	1.30	3⅜	3.10	5⅜	4.95	7⅜	6.75	9⅜	8.60
1½	1.40	3½	3.20	5½	5.05	7½	6.90	9½	8.70
1⅝	1.50	3⅝	3.35	5⅝	5.15	7⅝	7.00	9⅝	8.80
1¾	1.60	3¾	3.45	5¾	5.30	7¾	7.10	9¾	8.95
1⅞	1.75	3⅞	3.55	5⅞	5.40	7⅞	7.20	9⅞	9.05
2	1.85	4	3.70	6	5.50	8	7.35	10	9.15

AVAILABLE FABRIC WIDTHS

25″	65cm	50″	127cm
27″	70cm	54″/56″	140cm
35″/36″	90cm	58″/60″	150cm
39″	100cm	68″/70″	175cm
44″/45″	115cm	72″	180cm
48″	122cm		

AVAILABLE ZIPPER LENGTHS

4″	10cm	10″	25cm	22″	55cm
5″	12cm	12″	30cm	24″	60cm
6″	15cm	14″	35cm	26″	65cm
7″	18cm	16″	40cm	28″	70cm
8″	20cm	18″	45cm	30″	75cm
9″	22cm	20″	50cm		